A Guide to Hayling Island. ... Illustrated. (Second edition.).

Harry Richard Trigg

A GUIDE

TO

HAYLING ISLAND

WITH

HISTORICAL INCIDENTS

INCLUDING

A BRIEF ACCOUNT OF THE MOST INTERESTING SIGHTS WITHIN
A DAY'S JOURNEY, AND HOW TO GO TO THEM.

BY

H. R. TRIGG, F.A.I.

ILLUSTRATED.

LONDON
WATERLOW & SONS LIMITED, PRINTERS, LONDON WALL.

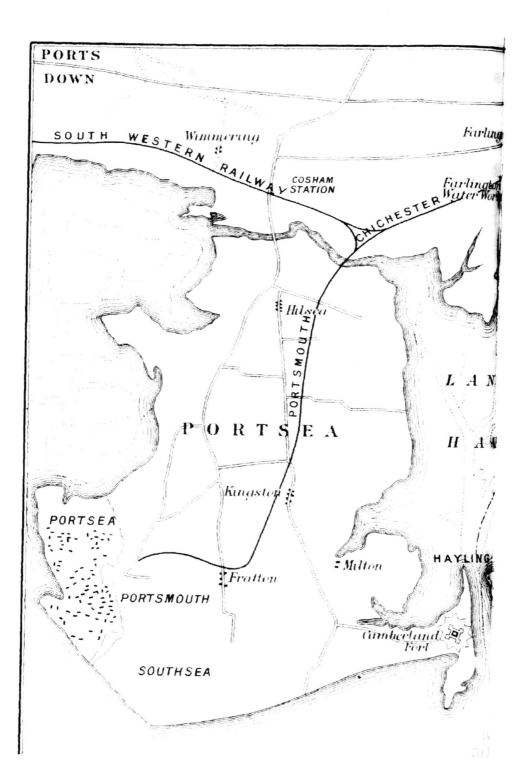

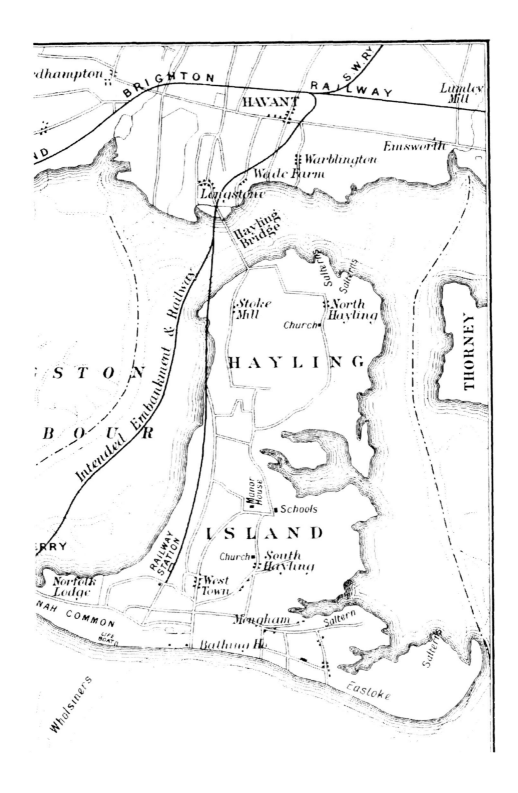

CONTENTS.

~~~~~~~~~~~~

INTRODUCTION.

THE rapid sale of my former work, the acquirement of earlier records and additional interesting information, have induced me to place before the reader a Second Edition, so compiled that he may trace the historical account of Hayling Island from its earliest known records to the present time.

1892.

GUIDE TO HAYLING ISLAND.

CHAPTER I.

Introductory.

Its Position—Means of Approach—Natural Beauty—Bathing—Balmy Air—Rides and Drives—View—Sands—Railway—Ferries—Hundred of Bosmere—Boulder Stones—Cultivation—Spring—Church—Inundation—Parish Register—Population.

HAYLING ISLAND is situated between the Counties of Hampshire and Sussex; it contains 7,531 acres, with a sea-frontage of about four and a half miles, with a S.S.W. aspect, facing the English Channel. The Map which accompanies the present edition will give a clear idea of its position. With reference to the immediate neighbourhood, the mode of access to it by rail is viâ Havant, either by the London and South Coast Railway, from Victoria, London Bridge, or any of its numerous other stations, or by the London and South Western Railway, from Waterloo Bridge, or from its numerous branches, which give ready communication with the Western Counties, viâ Cosham and Bishopstoke, to Bath, Bristol and Exeter, or from the North Western district viâ Salisbury. Its approach from Havant is either by the Hayling Railway, which crosses the Langston Harbour, and skirts the north-western shore of the island to South Hayling Station, or by a charming country drive of five miles through the village of Langston, over the wooden bridge erected in 1824, through the parish of North

Hayling, and thence through the most picturesque part of the Island to the South Beach. There is another approach viâ Portsmouth or Fratton Railway Stations, through the village of Milton, passing Fort Cumberland, crossing the Sinah Ferry, and landing on the most western shore of the Island.

It would be difficult to exaggerate the natural beauty of the Island, or its capability of being made a watering place as attractive in every respect as any other on the South Coast. It possesses a sea-frontage, available for building purposes, of upwards of four miles.* The beach is exceedingly beautiful, the sands at low water being so remarkably firm and dry. They afford a magnificent equestrian gallop of over three miles, and the bathing is acknowledged to be superior to that of any other part of the coast ; being entirely free from sea weed, the beach is exempt from the disagreeable nuisance and unsightliness of its decomposition. With a direct southern aspect to the sea, the Island enjoys, throughout the year, an extremely pure and balmy air; it is remarkably exempt from rain, and has a temperature so mild and genial, that vegetation is more advanced in spring and summer than in the most favoured parts of Surrey. Hayling is singularly free from land fogs, and is protected from the east winds by the projection of Selsea Bill; from the south-west winds by the Isle of Wight ; and from the north winds by the Portsdown Hill. There is, in fact, no seaside place in the South of England more richly endowed by nature, or better calculated to impart health and vigour to the frame. The healthiness of the district is chiefly to be attributed to the presence of the health-giving and invigorating Ozone contained in the atmosphere arising from the bed of the harbour after the sea has receded. It is this same Ozone, under similar circumstances, which has rendered Weston-super-Mare such a favourite resort. In a population of 1,138 in 1871, the number of deaths amounted only to 14, or 11½ in 1,000—the average

---

* The frontage of Brighton, Kemp Town, and Hove is not more than three miles and a half; the one beautifully curved, and the other straggling.

death-rate of Great Britain being 23 in 1000. In fact, no medical practitioner has hitherto been enabled to subsist upon the ailments of the residents at Hayling.

The beautiful turf upon the beach also affords a magnificent field for equestrian exercise in a grass gallop of nearly three miles. One of the most delightful features of the Island is its abundance of fine trees. The agreeable roads which traverse the place are shaded to a most remarkable extent, and the rides and drives to be obtained are such as are seldom met with on the sea coast. In this respect Hayling has more the charming aspect of a grove than of a plain and level country.

The sea view from the beach is one of the greatest attractions of the place. From an open offing to the south-west the eye ranges along the whole northern frontage of the Isle of Wight, the streets of Ryde being clearly visible with a glass of moderate power. The Solent and Spithead, with the fleet at anchor, and the newly-constructed forts, Fort Cumberland, Southsea, and the town of Portsmouth in the distance, form a beautiful picture, whilst steam and sailing vessels, yachts, and boats render the near view ever varied and attractive. The inland views are exceedingly picturesque, embracing a wide range from the Portsdown Hills to Chichester Cathedral, Wittering, and Selsea Bill.

The student of natural history will find many attractions at Hayling. Besides the variety of magnificent and venerable timber trees, the genial climate encourages a luxuriant growth of fruit and flowers, and the fields and hedge rows furnish a profusion of ferns; the sea affords a singular variety of fish; shells of great beauty, many of them rare, are frequently cast upon the beach; while most of our British birds, and many who visit us but rarely, are seen in their respective seasons in this little island.

The lover of field sports will here find facilities for their enjoyment. Game and rabbits are plentiful; whilst he who delights in wild fowl shooting will, in the winter time, find geese, widgeon, and other water fowl in abundance; the Hambledon Foxhounds meet in the vicinity, and Coursing meetings are of frequent occurrence.

An important feature of the place is the excellent supply of fresh water, which is abundant, and of the very best description. The springs are numerous, and many of them near the surface.

The extreme length of Hayling from north to south is about three miles five furlongs. Its width at the sea-frontage is about four miles ten chains, and, as it will be seen by the Map, it decreases very much in width to the northwards. About the centre of the Island its width is little more than five furlongs. Its total area is 7,531 acres.

The station of the Hayling Railway is a little over a quarter of a mile of the beach, on the western side of the Island. From this station seven trains run daily to and from Havant, and these are so timed as to meet the trains on the London and Brighton Railway to Portsmouth on the west; to Chichester, Bognor, Shoreham, Eastbourne, and Hastings on the east; and also by way of London and South Western, London, Woking, Guildford, Bishopstoke, Basingstoke, Reading, Salisbury, Windsor, &c. The distance from London is about 70 miles. There are several through trains either way daily, either by South Western or South Coast Railway, and the daily journey is performed in about two hours. From Havant to South Hayling the distance is five miles, which (stopping at Langston and North Hayling) is traversed in 15 minutes.

By the Map it will be seen that the Island has on its western side Langston Harbour, and to the east Chichester Harbour. Across the entrance to each of these there is a ferry. To the west the ferry conducts the passenger to the peninsula which is occupied by Portsmouth and Southsea. Landing at Cumberland Fort it is an easy walk to Southsea Beach and Pier, from whence there is ready access by steam boats to Ryde, Cowes, and Southampton. A tramway from the Southsea Pier affords a conveyance in less than a quarter of an hour to the Portsmouth Station of the Brighton and South Western Railways. The eastern ferry gives access to West Wittering and the main land, and by way of Chichester Harbour there is a pleasant water-way to Emsworth, Bosham, and Chichester.

All the principal features of Hayling Island will be more particularly mentioned in their respective places, and those of interest within a day's journey will be referred to.

Families desiring to spend their holidays at the sea-side for the sake of relaxation and health (without artificial gaiety) will find Hayling cannot be excelled. There are few places so eligible at all periods of the year; in winter the air is mild and salubrious, and full of restorative properties.

It is, of course, impossible to convey a complete idea of any place by mere description, but it may be hoped that the Map and the Illustrations which accompany these pages will enable the reader to follow our remarks.

The Island is in the Hundred of Bosmere, which includes also the Manors of Havant, Warblington, and Lymbourne, all to the northward of Hayling. When Hampshire, or the County of Southampton, was divided for administrative purposes Hayling became part of the Fareham division, which includes Fareham, Havant, Portsdown, Titchfield, and the adjacent country. Hampshire is in the ecclesiastical province of Canterbury and diocese of Winchester, and (with the Isle of Wight) constitutes the archdeaconry of Winchester. The county is divided into twenty-three parochial unions, and Hayling forms part of the Havant Union. The issue of each Poor and Highway Rate of North Hayling Parish is about ten pence in the pound, and that of the South Parish to one shilling, and occasionally eighteen-pence. The rates in Portsmouth are little less than ten shillings in the pound, and this fact alone should constitute a great inducement to invest in land and building on the Island.

For legislative purposes, Hayling is part of the southern division of Hampshire, which returns one Member of Parliament, the present representative being Lieut.-General Sir Frederick Wellington Fitzwygram, Bart., J.P., Leigh Park, Havant.

The Assizes for the county are held at Winchester twice in the year, the Quarter Petty Sessions at Havant, and the County Court—which sits monthly, or as frequently as may be necessary—at Portsmouth. The police arrangements are under Superintendent Littlefield, of the Fareham Division of the Hants Constabulary, who resides at Fareham.

Under the ancient charters, from Henry I. downwards, the inhabitants of Hayling are exempt from serving on juries at the Sessions and Assizes; and upon a question which arose some years since at Winchester with reference to the exemption, the late Mr. Padwick appeared by counsel, and future attendance was excused.

The geological formation of Hampshire is chalk, and the superincumbent strata, of Portsea and Hayling Islands, are occupied to a large extent by the London clay. Portsdown Hill is an outlying mass of chalk. A number of large boulder stones are found in all parts of the Island, some of considerable size, weighing over 2½ tons. Some assume they are relics of stone circles or cromlechs of the Druidical period. Taking into consideration the great variance in their size and the roundness of their edges, the most reliable theory is that they were deposited here during the glacial period, when rocks were carried aloft to be dropped when the approach of a genial age destroyed the dominion of the cold.

From the quantity of timber still remaining at Hayling, and the much greater quantity which it is known to have contained formerly, there is every reason to believe that it was originally a perfect forest. The north coppice in Hayling North is evidently part of an ancient wood; the same may be said of East Stoke and Southwood. Eastock, or Estoke, signifies East*wood*, as Northstoke signifies North*wood*, so called in after-times. The court-rolls indicate the existence of much more timber than there is now. At the beginning of the present century an avenue, which reached from the South Church to the Ham Farm, was felled; and it is stated that, not many years before, ten thousand pounds' worth of timber was cut and sold in a single season on the demesne lands of the Duke of Norfolk in the Island. At various times many fine trees have been thrown, by the violence of the wind; in the severe gale of 1866 over 300 trees were uprooted; at the same time a large rick house was lifted off its steadles and thrown against a barn, causing its complete destruction. That wild boar and

... er were formerly common in this forestal region, and included ... ghts of free warren exercised by the lords, is a proba- ... borated by authenticated facts in similar lands in ... f England. The "West*hay*" at Hayling, as it is ... old records, now corrupted into Westney, was ... dged or paled portion of a wood into which, beasts ... n were driven and captured. In Shropshire, Lancashire, ... ucestershire, Yorkshire, and other parts of England, ther... ...ere places termed *hays*, which were certainly applied to this purpose.

The cultivation of the Island consists chiefly of wheat, barley, and oats, succeeded by peas, tares, clover, and a small portion of trefoil. One or two farmers adopt the old-fashiond fallow system, the majority farming high, keeping sheep and rearing a large number of lambs, which are sent to London, Brighton, and the neighbouring markets. The land produces abundant and large root crops; wheat, barley, and oats are above the county average. There are several good orchards of delicious fruit; choice sorts of apples are plentiful, and arrive at great perfection. Honey is abundant.

There are numerous springs of excellent fresh water on the Island, varying considerably in depth. Near the Manor House, there is one called Sluts' Well, the water of which has never been known to fail, as it rises always to and generally overflows the adjoining surface. There is one spring upon the beach within a very short distance of the sea level at high water.

In early times Hayling was larger and of greater importance than at present. It comprised six tithings—Northney, Eastney, Stoke, Westney, Mengeham, and West Town, each representing ten families with their dependants, or a population of probably over one thousand, and, if we add the various towns which grew up subsequently, it is probable that in the fifteenth and sixteenth centuries the population of the Island was far greater than at present.

A submerged church stood about half-a-mile from the present line of the shore, almost facing the Royal Hotel, upon a spot known as the Church Rocks. It has been calculated that, prior to the great inundation, the Island

reached within two miles of the Nab light ship. (Th'⁓
no mean conjecture, for "Nimus" in his writings, refe⁓
the Isle of Wight, observes the Britains called it Gn'⁓
signifies a separation—which, as Deodorus Seculus '
at every tide it seemed to be an Island, but at th⁓'
ebb the ground between this Island and the *C* ⁓ɴ was
so dry, that the old Britons used to carry th ᴛʜɪɴɢs over
thither in carts.) If this statement be correct ᴛʜe devastation
must have swept away a space of some six or seven miles
long by five in breadth. The channel between Hayling and
Havant has become deeper within the last century. Old
persons have been heard to say that a man on horseback could
ride across at almost any time of tide, by jumping his horse
across the channel at the Wade-way. Within the past 25 years
the entrance to Chichester Harbour was only 295 yards wide
at high-water; the present T. Harris, Esq., used often to swim
his horse across whe⁓ coming from Whittering to Hayling.
This entrance is now ove⁓ mile wide. Within the past 10 years
over 20 acres of land ha⁓ ⁓n washed away from the south-
east end of the Island, wi⁓ ⁓he same space of time on the
opposite coast at Whitteri⁓ ⁓ds of 300 acres have been
devastated by the sea.

The parish registers con⁓ ⁓ 571, and from this date
they have been kept in orc⁓ ⁓ew pages are missing.
The several registers commn⁓

Nᴏʀᴛʜ Hᴀʏʟɪɴɢ.	Sᴏᴜᴛʜ Hᴀʏʟɪɴɢ.
For Births . . 1571	For Births . . 1672
„ Marriages . 1571	„ Marriages . 1672
„ Burials . . 1571	„ Burials . . 1672

From perusal of the ancient records in Chapter II. it will
be seen that the population of the Island fluctuated very much;
recent returns show a steady increase.

POPULATION AND HOUSES RECORDED.

Date.	Parish.	Houses.	Males.	Females.	Total.	For the whole Island.
1788	N. Hayling	...	...	...	285	536
	S. ,,	...	...	...	251	
1801	N. ,,	96	...	...	...	578
	S. ,,		...	...	...	
1851	N. ,,	61	...	...	272	1,096
	S. ,,	162	...	...	824	
1861	N. ,,	60	...	...	262	1,038
	S. ,,	163	372	404	776	
1871	N. ,,	61	143	138	281	1,138
	S. ,,	180	417	440	875	
1881	N. ,,	...	134	134	268	1,242
	S. ,,	247	497	577	1,074	
1891	N. ,,	80	139	139	278	1,495
	S. ,,	305	541	676	1,217	

The present rateable value in the south parish is £6,692 19s. 6d., and that of the north £2,183 9s. 3d.

Langston Harbour is safe and convenient, but its advantages are somewhat lessened by a bar of shifting sand called the Woolsinars (more properly the Woolsinar, or Shingle Bank) at some distance outside the entrance. The trade of the harbour is chiefly in coals, timber, bricks, malt, barley, oats, wheat, and other agricultural produce. This, as well as Chichester Harbour, is frequented by numerous vessels, the largest being of about 300 tons. The chief supply of coals comes direct by sea from Sunderland. Inland coals are also brought by railway.

The roads in Hayling were laid out centuries ago in the most convenient routes for intercourse with the churches, the manor houses, the ferries, the mill, the salterns, and other centres of devotion and business, and they are all in fair, and most of them in excellent condition. At the north extremity of the Island the principal road leads to the bridge* and

* By a private Act the bridge, with its quay dues, was purchased by the London and Brighton Railway Company.

causeway. The former is constructed of wood and iron, with an opening of 20 feet in the middle, to admit of the passage of large vessels at high water, and the causeway at each end of it is substantially built on piles.

The western ferry, at the entrance to Langston Harbour, has a width of about 300 yards at high water. The point of departure from the Island is called Sinah Point, and the toll for passengers from thence to the beach at Cumberland Fort is twopence each way to strangers, and one penny to the Islanders.* The ferry is not available for cattle, vehicles or heavy goods.

Various plans have from time to time been prepared to obtain a better communication between the Island and Southsea; the first of these was a floating bridge, similar to that plying between Portsmouth and Gosport. This was abandoned, when a gigantic scheme was placed before Parliament, and an Act obtained to join South Hayling Station with Fratton, crossing the Langston Harbour by an iron bridge, so constructed to form traffic as a road and railway bridge. The necessary grants of land were obtained from the Admiralty and the Board of Trade. Disputes in reference to the Common regulation (hereafter referred to) caused the scheme to be abandoned, and the Act lapsed. The most recent attempt to obtain the desired communication has been to construct a free bridge, to be built of iron on the telescopic principle. A large and influential meeting, with A. G. Sandeman, Esq., as chairman, was held at the Royal Hotel on 23rd October, 1891. Plans of the proposed bridge and its estimated cost ($£20,000$) were produced at the meeting, and a committee was formed to work, in union with the inhabitants of Portsmouth, to carry out the scheme, of so great importance to the two places. This would inevitably be soon supplemented by omnibus or tramway communication from Southsea to Hayling Beach.

---

* It was sold by the Lord of the Manor to a private company (Messrs. Sandeman, McEvan, and others) in 1875 for the ostensible purpose of providing a floating bridge with suitable accommodation for vehicular and other traffic.

The importance of this to the inhabitants of Hayling, Southsea and Portsmouth cannot be over-rated.

The eastern ferry crossing Chichester Harbour is worked by the Preventive service men, whose boats are at the extreme eastern shore of Eastoke.

The railway time tables show there is ready communication by train to and from Havant and Portsmouth. Omnibuses and other traps convey passengers and luggage to and from the Hayling Railway Station to the Royal Hotel and other places on the arrival and departure of each train. Our subsequent pages will supply the reader with information as to the means of access by steamboat from Southsea Pier to Ryde, Cowes, Gosport, and Southampton. There are frequent trips round the Isle of Wight in the summer, and pleasure boats may be hired on the Island for sailing in the bay. Langston Harbour affords excellent mooring ground for yachts.

The Guardian of North and South Hayling, together with others of the Havant Union, constitute the Rural Sanitary Authority for South Hayling and Warblington. Medical Officer of Health, Mr. W. Norman, Havant. Building Surveyor, Mr. H. R. Trigg, Hayling South. Inspector of Nuisances, Mr. E. Carrell, Havant. Registrar of Births, Deaths and Marriages, Mr. Briant, Havant.

The first church erected in the Island was that mentioned in William's grant to the Abbey of Jumièges, probably erected about the year 1040 by the Abbey of Winchester, who became possessed of Hayling by the gift of Queen Emma.

The precise site of this building, which was gradually submerged in the great inundations in the fourteenth century, is supposed to be marked by the existing Church Rocks, more than half a mile to the south of the present shore of Hayling; the portion of an ancient font in South Hayling Church is now to be found near the pulpit, placed upon stones which formed a part of the present church piers before the recent restoration, it was discovered in a shallow well in the south parish about the year 1826, is probably a relic of this first church, being exactly similar, in general design and ornamentation, to other fonts admitted to be anterior to the

2

Conquest. In this font the earliest converts to Christianity within the Island may be assumed to have received their baptism; and it is, therefore, one of the most ancient and interesting relics of antiquity of which the Island can boast.

Though nominally divided into two parishes, as North and South Hayling, with a church in each, the Island forms practically only one parish, the tithe commutation rent-charge being based upon 3,560 acres of land. Miss F. Padwick is the Lay Rector; the Rev. C. H. Clark, B.A., is vicar of St. Mary's, South Hayling, and perpetual curate of St. Peter's, North Hayling. He was presented to the living in 1889 by Miss F. Padwick. The Rev.   is curate. On the Sunday, service is held in the South Church at 10.30 a.m. and 6 p.m., and at the North Church at 10.30 a.m. and 6 p.m., alternately, and 2.30 on other Sundays.

The Holy Communion is administered on the first two Sundays in each month, and on the great festivals; Baptism at afternoon service, any Sunday; Churchings after evening service. Fees: Publication of banns, 1s.; certificate of marriage, 1s.; marriage after banns, 5s., clerk, 2s. 6d.; by licence, 10s., clerk, 5s. Burials, plain grave, parishioners, 1s.; non-parishioners, 7s. 8d.; setting up headstone, 10s.; brick graves and vaults according to size.

The accompanying illustration represents the interesting and beautiful structure of St. Mary's Church, South Hayling.

It is adapted by its size for a much larger population than the Island possesses, and comprises a nave with side aisles and a chancel, a tower or lantern at the junction of the nave and chancel, surmounted by a steeple covered with shingles, and a beautiful porch on the south side of the nave. The nave is 63 feet long by 45 feet wide, including the aisles. The pillars separating the nave from the aisles are octagonal, some of the capitals being foliated. There are three lancet windows in either aisle, deeply splayed with depressed arches in the interior. At the east end of the south aisle is an oratory containing a trefoil piscina, and the arches of this oratory differ from those of nave and tower. The corbels from which they spring are highly decorated; that on the south side, beneath a fretwork capital, bears the head of a crowned

female, and that on the northern side, beneath a capital ornamented with fleur-de-lis, above a wreath of ivy leaves, bears the head of a crowned man. These are supposed to represent Edward I. and Eleanor of Castile, and to fix the date of the work as between 1272 and 1291, the latter being the year in which Queen Eleanor died. One of the interior corbels of the western doorway of the nave represents a serpent, and the other a horn. A clerestory, with small quatrefoil windows, occupies the space between the arches and the roof. The font, now used for baptisms, stands near the western door. It is of stone and of square form, resting upon a central and four angle columns, the capitals of which are formed of sculptured heads. This appears to be a work of the twelfth century, and therefore older than the church itself. It may possibly have been brought from the Priory at its dissolution. The fragment of a still older font has been already mentioned.

The tower or lantern, which rises between the nave and chancel, is 24 feet square, the arches supporting it being good specimens of early decorated work. Upon the base stones are some fine specimens of carving in excellent preservation. The groove for the screen is still visible, and the brackets which once supported the rood-loft also remain on the imposts of the arch. Formerly there was a flight of steps leading to the belfry, which originally contained four bells, one of which bore the date 1324. Of these only one now remains, the others having been sold in 1805 for £170, to provide for some repairs of the church. The bell now in the tower has the following inscription upon it, " In God is my hope, 1673." It also has a representation of a 1s. piece of Charles the First, The steeple was re-shingled in June, 1734, at a cost of £42. and again in the year 1771.

The chancel is 42 feet long by 18 feet wide, and very lofty. The eastern windows consist of five lancet openings, united. There are three windows on each side of the chancel, deeply splayed and raised high above the ground. In the southern wall is a double trefoil piscina. In the floor of the chancel are two stone coffin lids ; one of them with a crosier upon it is ascribed to one of the priors of Hayling.

The south porch is spacious and beautiful in its design, being constructed of open work in oak. It has two seats, and before the recent restoration was partly paved with ancient stone coffin-lids. These have been replaced with tiles to correspond with those of the nave.

The nave window was blown in by the great storm of January, 1734, and replaced in the same year by a very common-placed window at a cost of £52. 15s.

In the year 1868 the church, with the exception of the chancel, was restored under the superintendence of Mr. G. E. Street, R.A., the architect of the New Law Courts in London, in whose able hands, it is scarcely necessary to say, the original features of the building were carefully adhered to. Whilst removing the rubbish for the new floor, remnants of the original nave window were discovered; these were placed together, the window of 1734 was taken out, and one after the original design placed in its present position.

The stone carvings have been brought up to their original sharpness; the floor has been re-laid with excellent red tiles, laid diagonally and separated by bands of tiles of a dark colour; the roof has been substantially repaired, and new open seats have been provided. The cost of restoration, which was raised by subscription, amounted to £1,705.

Near the junction of the nave and chancel a stone pulpit (designed by Mr. G. E. Street) has been erected at the cost of Mrs. Sandeman, the widow of Mr. G. G. Sandeman, who was a large contributor to the restoration.

In July, 1872, this steeple was struck by lightning. Some of the massive oaken timbers in the interior were completely split asunder. The lightning struck the steeple on the north-west side, passing completely through it and the belfry, and going out nearly at the base of the tower at the south-west angle, displacing a large piece of the water table of the roof, which was driven with great force on to the roof of the south aisle. The damage done was not considerable, and a fund was raised by subscription to make it good, a lightning conductor being now fitted to the steeple.

Until 1873 no permanent arrangement was made for lighting the church during the dark days and evenings of winter,

and it was the practice, both here and at the North Church, for the members of the congregation to take their own candles with them. In that year, however, Mr. W. Culliford originated a subscription by means of which paraffin lamps where provided for the South Church.

In 1882, through the energy of the Rev. J. A. Bell, the vicar, the oil lamps were taken away and the church lit with gas.

For some years the columns of the nave and the caps supporting the clerestory had shown weakness, but the earthquake of 1889, which was plainly felt on the Island, caused considerable damage, and in 1891 it was found necessary to remove them. Granite was used to replace the original stone. Other restorations were then made, and the church warmed by hot air, at a total outlay of about £500.

Close to the south porch is an immense yew tree, perhaps one of the finest in the country, which is shown in our illustration of the church. The yew, as is well-known, is an evergreen tree, a native of Europe, and indigenous to nearly every part of Great Britain and Ireland; it seldom grows in company with its own species, but generally alone, or with trees of a different kind. It does not attain a great height; at three or four feet from the ground numerous spreading branches shoot from the trunk, forming a head of close foliage, which, when fully grown, rises 30 or 40 feet from the ground, and continues to grow for about 100 years.

The most ancient yew tree, with greatest girth, may be found in the churchyard of the picturesque village of Barcombe, in Sussex. It stands in good preservation near the porch.

The finest avenue of yews we have in Hampshire is that at Chilton Candover, about half a mile long, the trees being still in a vigorous state of growth, although probably four or five hundred years old. In Upper Clatford churchyard, near Andover, there is a fine old yew tree with thirteen separate trunks, all undoubtedly growing from the old shell. In Corhampton churchyard there is a yew tree, said to be a thousand years old, which is about 22 feet round and as fresh as ever. In Selborne churchyard there is a yew the trunk of which is 23 feet 8 inches in circumference. Yews were often planted in churchyards to protect the churches from violent winds, and they were often resorted to for bows. Shakespere often mentions the yew, and always of a tree of ill-omen—as in "King Richard III.":—

> The very headsmen learn to bend their bows
> Of double-fatal yew against thy state.

Classic authors have frequently referred to the supposed poisonous properties of the yew tree, and some of them state that its shade is fatal to those who sleep under it, but modern observation has dispelled these notions as erroneous. Our old poets and chroniclers abound with references to the use of the branches of the yew for bows before, and indeed long after, the introduction of gunpowder.

The yew tree in Hayling churchyard has long had its main branches supported by massive props. Its girth, at a height of four feet from the ground, is 31 feet; the diameter of the space covered by its spreading branches is 62 feet, and one of its limbs has a circumference of nine feet. Its age is a matter of pure conjecture, in all probability much older than the church; it may even date from the days when Harold and the Norman Conqueror took forcible possession of the Island.

The churchyard covers a space of about two acres, exclusive of the church. The southern and northern portions were devoted to the interment of parishioners of South and North Hayling respectively. The northern fence of the churchyard was formerly kept in repair by the north parish, the western hedge by the owners of certain lands in West Town, six panels of paling by the owner of Manor Farm, four by the owner of Eastoke Farm, and the remainder by other landed proprietors. The tombstones are neither very numerous nor remarkable. One, dated 1767, to the memory of John Jacob, has a rude basso-relievo of a ship with two figures, one bearing an anchor and the other a trident, and probably intended as representations of Hope and Neptune. Near the west end of the church is a monument to the memory of George Glas Sandeman, Esq., late of London and Westfield, South Hayling, who was born at Perth, October 20, 1792, and died in London, January 9, 1868. This consists of a pedestal of granite,

surmounted by a representation of rock-work, carrying a large ornamental cross of polished granite. The whole is surrounded by granite pedestals at equal distances apart, connected by ornamental chains.

There are a few curious epitaphs, one to William Bayley, the village blacksmith, who died in 1760—

> My sledge and hammer lie reclined,
> My bellows, too, have lost their wind,
> My fire extinct, my forge decayed,
> And in the dust my vice is laid ;
> My coal is spent, my iron gone,
> My nails are drove, my work is done.

Another to Thomas Abbut, for many years the Hayling ferryman, who died November, 1762—

> No more I ply my oars from side to side,
> Nor dread the blustering storm or raging tide ;
> My boat is now safe moored, all labour cease ;
> Christ is my Anchor, and I rest in peace.

To the eastward of the church is a piece of land containing about a quarter of an acre, called "Surplice Plot," which was formerly held on the tenure of washing the vicar's surplices three times a year, a service which is now commuted to three half-crowns. Amongst the other claims made the subject of litigation by the late lord of the manor, Mr. Padwick, was one to the freehold of this plot. This he succeeded in gaining, but his successor, Mr. Osmond Barnard, on purchasing the manor, restored it to the vicar and churchwardens in perpetuity.

The old vicarage stood in a field known as the "Vicarage Field," about 300 yards to the south of St. Mary's Church, a venerable remnant of Tudor architecture.

The new vicarage house, about three-quarters of a mile from the South Church, is a substantial modern residence built upon a portion of the glebe. There are about 30 acres of glebe land attached to the vicarage, most of which is arable. The value of the vicarage is estimated at £300 per annum.

About three miles to the northward of the South Hayling Church is the Church or Chapel of Ease of North Hayling, represented in the accompanying illustration. This in the old records is called the Chapel of St. Peter (to whom it was dedicated) at Northwood, in Hayling, and the hamlet in which it stands is still known as Hayling Northwood.

This building is of greater antiquity than the South Church, and was doubtless a chapel of ease to the original church submerged by the inundations. It is a plain edifice of simple early English architecture, apparently dating from the reign of Henry II. (1140 to 1190). It consists, like the South Church, of a nave and aisles, and a chancel with a low turret at the junction of the two main portions of the building. Its entire length is only 60 feet, and the width of the nave and aisles is 30 feet. There is a good west window of the decorated period. The aisles are separated from the nave by massive columns and plain pointed arches. Over the capital of one of the columns on the south are remains of an ancient fresco-painting of armorial bearings in red colour, in one of the quarterings of which is a fleur-de-lis. The nave is paved with old red tiles, and has carved oak open seats with finials, which are hollowed for the reception of candles to light the church. There is an ancient font on the south side of the nave. The north aisle has a trefoil-headed niche to the east for an altar, over which is a pedestal, which doubtless formerly supported an image. There was formerly an open timber roof from the west end to the chancel, of which one of the principals is yet to be traced, the lower part being visible from below, and an upper part of it being concealed in the belfry. This appears to have been somewhat elaborately carved. In the turret are three fine and very ancient bells, one of which bears the inscription, "Sancta Maria ora pro nobis." The steeple, which is very low and covered with shingles, is comparatively modern. The chancel has a piscina and an ambry, and contains an old carved surplice chest, and it was separated from the body of the church by a screen, a portion of which still remains. On the north is a small carved wooden porch. This church has recently gone under repairs. Many points of interest and beauty have been restored, at a cost of £1,150.

In the fifteenth century Waynflete, Bishop of Winchester, directed the Vicar of Hayling to find a chaplain at Northwood, and the parishioners to find a house for him, and he also determined the proportions in which the repairs of the chapel should be borne by the respective parties. The parishioners accordingly built a residence for the chaplain, which in modern times was called the vicarage house, and this, after being tenanted by paupers, fell into a state of dilapidation, and was pulled down in 1828. The Vicar of Hayling still receives thirty shillings a year from the church-wardens. The chancels of both churches are now repaired by Miss F. Padwick, who is the Lay Rector of both parishes.

At Stoke is the oldest dwelling on the Island, dating probably from the days of the Plantagenets. The house has been substantially repaired by Mr. W. C. Turner, the owner. Not far from the above is a field, called the " Towncil Field," in all probability the site of a Roman villa or council house. By permission of Mr. Dilnot, the present owner of the land, Mr. H. R. Trigg made some slight excavations, in which were found a bronze ring, a spear head, a quantity of disturbed Roman tessellated pavement, remnants of Roman pottery, the prevailing colour being a grayish black, dark drab and red glazed samian with relief ornamentation. In dry summers the outline of this building, which is one hundred and thirty-one feet long by sixty-three feet wide, together with the internal walls, can clearly be traced by the defective growth of the crops over the foundation; foundations of other buildings can in the same way be found. In the adjacent field a sepulchral urn, 12 inches high by 10 inches wide, was unearthed. In digging out for a water-course some few years since in the neighbourhood, two unique Roman plates were found. They are now in the possession of Mr. W. C. Turner, who also has portions of kern and other remains of antiquity.

On the north-west shore of the Island evidence exists which warrants the supposition that pottery of various kinds was made there by the Romans, from the quantity of fragments that may be found, and the number of pot-holes to be seen indicate that a yard of considerable size was established here. In subsequent years the sea wall has been repaired by the refuse from the above yard. To the present time no trace of any kiln has been found. A Roman wine cooler and other kerns have been found. We may infer that the before-mentioned villa and yard may have been deserted by the Romans in 577, when the cities of Bath, Gloucester, and Silchester were overthrown by the victorious armies of Ceasilon of Wessex.

Close to North Hayling Railway Station stand the remains of a well-established windmill. It was thoroughly repaired a few years since, and worked two pairs of stones; it was destroyed by fire in October, 1890.

The views from this portion of the Island are exceedingly attractive, including the Portsdown Hills, Langston Harbour, and the adjoining country to the north.

Near the middle of the Island, on its eastern side, is a deep bay or inlet, nearly seven acres in extent, which forms the feeding pond for a large tidal mill which had existed for many centuries, and the extent of which points, with other evidence, to a greater population in former ages than the present. The tide as it rose was admitted to the feeding pond by flood-gates, which were closed at high water, and the ebbing of this water turned a large water-wheel. In 1876 Mr. F. Padwick restored the mill, which had been much dilapidated, providing a new water-wheel with iron fans and wooden floats, and also a new driving wheel and new tackle throughout. Three pairs of mill stones were worked in the preparation of pollard, middlings, and sharps. Large quantities of oak timber had been skilfully employed in the internal construction of the mill.

A drying-kiln and store rooms were attached to the mill; the miller's house contains five rooms, and the out-buildings comprise a stable, granary, and pig-styes. The mill-pond, mill-plot, and paddock occupy in all an area of 15 acres. This interesting and venerable water-mill is shown in the accompanying illustration. With regret I have to record the total destruction of this ancient water-mill by fire, 5th January, 1877, the origin of which is wrapped in mystery; the remains of the mill are still to be seen, and referred to A.D. 1294.

The Parochial Schools near the Pound were erected under the approval of the London School Board, from the plans prepared by Mr. H. R. Trigg, at a cost of £1,350; this sum, through the indefatigable exertions of the Rev. C. Hardy, was raised by public subscriptions. The schools are now

under the control of a committee, with the Rev. C. H. Clark as chairman. The site of the school was presented by F. Padwick, Esq., of Thorney Island, the present owner of the Manor Farm.

The principal farm in Hayling is the Manor Farm, which occupies a nearly central position in the Island. In the particulars of the last sale by auction it was described as comprising about 693 acres of land, of which about 541 were arable, 152 pasture, 77 wood, 14 acres brickfields, 15 acres mill, land, house, and water.

The land on the farm is a deep loam, highly productive, and in a good state of cultivation. The Manor of Hayling was at the same time described as follows :—The Manor of Hayling, with its extensive rights and privileges under various grants from the Crown, with 53 copyhold tenants, 670 acres of copyhold land, with buildings thereon, presumed annual value of about £1,500. Under suit of court and other services by payment of arbitrary fines, computed at the rate of two years' value on each change of tenant, by death and alimation, and a heriot consisting of the best beast or best chattel for each tenement. The quit rents amount to about £23 per annum. The Manor includes the rights of soil of the Common of Gutner,* Eastoke,* Vernor, and North Common,* with the timbers thereon, and the rights of wreck on the sea shore and of free warren.

Gutner Common has since been sold as freehold property. Vernor Common, the only one in which the lord established his right, has been enclosed by consent of those holding the right of cowlease over it, the lord and the cowleasers taking their respective portions.

The Manor House is a large brick-built house, approached by a carriage drive through ornamental grounds. There is an entrance hall, with seven large reception rooms on the ground floor, ten bed-rooms above, and excellent domestic offices. There is stabling attached for eight horses ; good gardens, and

---

* These were severally disputed, and at the time of the completion of the sale a sum of £400 was allowed to Mr. O. Barnard, through the apparent want of title to this and the right of wreck upon the shore at Eastoke.

farm homestead.   The house, which was built in 1777, by the then Duke of Norfolk, lord of the manor, is now occupied by Miss Padwick.

Near to the Manor House on the west is the old Tithe Barn of the Manor, which is remarkable for its magnitude, antiquity, and construction.   It is no less than 140 feet in length, by 40 in width, and therefore occupies a much larger area than the South Church.   It is lofty in proportion, and light almost to elegance in the arrangement of the old English oaken supports which divide it, as it were, into a nave and aisles.   The thatched roof has been carefully renewed from time to time; the walls are brick upon a stone basement, probably as old as the fourteenth century.   This barn is capable of holding upwards of 150 loads of sheaf wheat.

Until within the last few years there was, close to the great barn just described, a smaller barn, built from a cargo of German oak (wrecked some centuries ago) by one of the ancestors of the Duke of Norfolk, as lord, and appropriated to this purpose.   The tradition is that the oak was shipped from the Elbe, and intended for a monastery in France.

The dovecote of the former grange (which occupied the site of the Manor House) was in existence so lately as 1857, and was capable of containing a vast number of pigeons.   The walls were of great thickness, and perforated for the ingress and egress of the birds.*

Near the entrance to the grounds of the Manor House is the parish pound, and just opposite is an enclosure, now overgrown with trees and underwood, which contains a well-built dog-kennel, where the late Mr. Padwick kept his hounds, but this has now gone to decay.

In this neighbourhood are some of the new and improved labourers' cottages, erected by the Mr. Padwick who, as explained in the preceding chapter, is now the owner of the Manor Farm.

* It was held in the case of Boulston v. Hardy (Cro. Eliz. 548) that dovecotes could be erected by the lord of a manor only, and that if a private person erected a dovecote, he was punishable in the court-leet for a nuisance.   It was clearly a manorial privilege in early times, and formed a considerable item of profit and convenience to the lord.

The Sunday Schools, near the Manor House, belong to Mrs. Parry, and are let to the parish at the nominal rent of £6 1s. a year, which is returned as an annual subscription.

About half a mile from the South Church on the east side of the Island is a place called Tourner Bury, as to the origin and purposes of which various suppositions have been entertained.

It occupies a rising ground, forming almost a circular vallum; the diameter at its greatest width is about one-seventh of a mile; it is surrounded by a fosse, the vallum being about six feet high, and the fosse originally of the same depth; but time has lessened the depth of the latter, the banks having washed into it and partially filled it up with leaves and decayed vegetable matter.

The interior space contains about three acres, and the furrows across it show that it was at one time under cultivation; there is timber upon it of recent growth, and upon the sides of the vallum are several oak and yew trees, perhaps coeval with the formation of the embankment. No traces of any building, no bones or fragments of any kind to testify its purpose, have, however, yet been found within this space to show its origin or appropriation.

The word " Tourn " in ancient times signified the sheriff's court, from attendance upon which only archbishops, bishops, abbots, priors, earls, barons, all religious men and women, and all such as had hundreds of their own, were exempt. " Bury " signified a town or enclosed place. The tourn was the great court-leet of the county, of which the sheriff was the judge. It was enacted by Magna Charta that no sheriff should make his tourn through a hundred but twice in the year, namely, once after Easter and once after the feast of St. Michael.

The sheriff authority extended to treason and felonies by the common law, as well as to the lowest offences against the King, such as seizure of treasure trove, estrays, wrecks, &c., common nuisances, as selling victuals unfit for food, breaking the assize of bread and beer, keeping false weights and measures, and disturbances against the peace. By the common law, originally all men of the neighbourhood were

bound to be present upon every inquiry, whether of robbery
or any other offence. These large assemblies were necessarily
held in the open air. About the reign of Henry III., however,
these general attendances ceased to be required, and a sworn
jury acted for the public body. To a very late period the
justices-itinerant held their assize in the Strand of London,
sitting on the stone steps by Somerset House. A somewhat
similar practice still exists in the Isle of Man.

Thornbury, on the banks of the Severn, in Gloucestershire,
was the place at which the sheriff's tourn was held in former
days, and the name of that place is remarkable in similarity to
that of Tourner Bury in the Isle of Hayling. The sheriff's
tourn was held in Hayling down to the year 1781. As a
further illustration of the origin and progress of Tourner Bury,
the "Saxon Chronicle" records that the Saxon Viking,
Ella, and his three sons, landed A.D. 477 at West Wittering,
in Sussex, about a mile distant from Hayling. It is a singular
confirmation of this fact that a spot there still retains the
name of Ellanor, given, no doubt, by the invaders to the shore
where their intrepid leader commenced his career of conquest,
for, it is added, "that they there slew many Britons, and
dispersed many into the wood Andred." The same chronicle
tells us further that A.D. 490 Ella and his son Cissa besieged
Chichester, about seven miles distant, and slew all the inhabitants, so that not one Briton was left.

It is reasonable to suppose that between these two dates,
and afterwards, the Saxons remained in the vicinity of their
first landing. Hayling Island presented a most favourable
spot for their location. Lying under the lee of the Isle of
Wight—well-wooded, as is testified by the terms north-wude
and south-wude, into which the island is still divided—
accessible by water only, and on three sides of it defended at
low water by an extensive tract of yielding mud—having water
communication with the main land nearly to Chichester on
the one hand, and to Portchester and the localities to the
westward on the other hand—of great fertility, and with other
advantages to maritime adventurers which are obvious—it
would have been impossible to select a place better adapted
for the establishment of the invaders. That they did occupy

and cultivate the Island cannot be doubted. They have left their mark in the names still borne by numerous spots. Thus we are able, by their unchanged Saxon appellations, to point out the inhabited village, their sheep pasture, the brooklands, covered with sedge and fern, the regal residence, where justice was administered in public assembly, and even the hawthorn (hœkthorn) row, which exists still. But the spot most interesting to the antiquary is Tourner Bury. It was, as its compound name implies, a stronghold, placed under the protection of Thor or Thuror. The venerable yew trees yet growing around it bear witness alike to its antiquity and to its dedication, and a survey will show at a glance its purpose and its strength. The encampment covers a space of about seven acres, and is as nearly circular as the locality permitted. It stands on a spot of land jutting near the entrance of Chichester Harbour. In recent times a considerable portion of mud land in front of it has been reclaimed from the sea. When Tourner Bury was erected as a stronghold, it was protected on three sides by the tidal waters and the treacherous mud they covered. The ground around was artificially and carefully sloped to form a glacis, and surrounding the encampment itself was a deep fosse and vallum; the former below high-water level, and consequently with all the protection both of a permanent moat and a precipitous embankment. There was also a stockade, such as the New Zealanders erect round their pahs, and which were in use in this country so lately as the Battle of Hastings; and we may well believe that this place of defence must have been, in the then condition of the science of war, not alone of great strength, but one at that time well nigh impregnable. There was also a land winding or causeway, which enabled the defenders to cross the mud at low water, and so reach their boats or ships at Dip, or Deep "Rythe" at any time of tide, and capable of an easy defence similar to the celebrated causeway which was the scene of tragedy to the special invaders of Mexico on the terrible occasion known in history as the "Noche Triste" or "Night of Sadness."

Probably, at a later period, Tourner Bury was again occupied as a place of refuge and defence, as we know, upon the authority of the ancient chronicler, Rudborne, that in 1071 the Britons, being grievously oppressed by their Norman conquerors, appointed an indefatigable man, Hereward, as their leader, and, flying to the Islands of Hayling and Thorney, there entrenched themselves within strong defences.

It may be added that, in a field a short distance from Tourner Bury there exists a mound, supposed popularly to be the site of an ancient windmill. That is probably an error, since windmills are not usually so built, and the mound in question is too small for the purpose. It was apparently a barrow or burial place. Some thirty years ago, the field being drained, the labourer who dug the drains found a quantity of pottery under the surface of this mound, but, as it was broken, it attracted no attention. Most likely they were the remnants of sacrificial vessels, buried with a Saxon warrior chief close to the stormy waters which he loved, and, it may be, the scene of daring achievements, and an honoured though bloody death.

A short distance beyond Tourner Bury is a brickfield in full work. This has been established about fifty years, for the utilisation of the excellent brick-earth on the Island. It occupies about fourteen acres, and is let to Mr. John Durben. The bricks produced are of a superior description, and many millions of them have been sent to West Worthing and the Isle of Wight, for the erection of Government buildings.

In the southern portion of the island there is an Independent chapel, of which Mr. Cadoux is the minister.

East of this are to be found the remains of one of the five salterns there were at Hayling, viz., the great and little saltern in the north parish, and Mengham, Jenmans, and the Eastoke saltern in the south parish. The largest of these was the Mengham saltern. Domesday Book informs us that in the eleventh century a saltern was here which paid six shillings and eightpence. The Mengham saltern has been in use until recently. In former times these salterns were of great importance to the manorial lords, priors, and monks, both for the curing of fish and salting of beeves.

A considerable quantity of salt was here produced by evaporating the sea-water in shallow beds, and sent to Portsmouth, Chichester and other places in the neighbourhood.

The manufacture of salt is spoken of by St. Ambrose in 370 as follows :—" Let us consider those things which are common to many and expressive of the divine favour, how water is turned into salt of such substance as frequently to be cut with a knife. This is not uncommon in the British salt, which have both the solidity and glossy whiteness of marble, and are very wholesome."

The fishing in the Bay and Langston and Chichester Harbours affords constant occupation to an industrious portion of the native population of Hayling, Emsworth, Fishbourne, Milton, &c., and, in addition to the ordinary " harvest of the sea," this laborious class realises a special harvest every summer in the famous mackerel of Hayling Bay. The mackerel fishery on the southern side of the Island commences about the beginning of June, if wind and weather permit, and the season continues, if there are no strong winds on land, for a month or six weeks ; but it not unfrequently happens that their appearance is delayed until the beginning of July. The fish are first observed a considerable distance from the land, which they approach in such prodigious shoals that many thousands have sometimes been taken at a single haul. The time of fishing is from sunset to sunrise, and they are taken with a long draw-net of an inch and half mesh, from forty to fifty fathoms in length. One man stands on the shore holding the rope, while two others row off the boat and drop the net into the sea, which is afterwards drawn on shore. In the season the fish are sold for about one penny each ; they are from five to nine inches in length, and are considered the finest on the English coast. From their extreme delicacy they travel badly, and to be eaten in perfection they should be dressed within a few hours after they are taken out of the water.

During the fishing season of 1873, which was generally a very successful one, a large sturgeon was taken by William Goldring, and purchased by the Brighton Aquarium Company. It was safely removed there, but died from injuries sustained in the journey by railway.

Oysters of excellent quality have for many years been dredged from our harbours for the London and other markets up to 1868, when these delicious bivalves became suddenly scarce.   It was no uncommon thing to see, at the commencement of the season, a fleet of from 40 to 50 crafts from Whitstable, Colchester, Emsworth, Portsmouth, and other places, dredging in our harbours.

The reported success attending the artificial breeding of oysters at the Ile de Ré, and other parts of France, attracted considerable attention from men of science in England, as well as from speculators and dealers in that delicious bivalve, which, from the earliest period of history, has been a famous product of our coasts; and when, from its sudden and extreme scarcity, the oyster became an expensive luxury, the Legislature adopted some measures for the encouragement of the Oyster Fishery, and Joint Stock Companies were formed for increasing the supply, by preserving the annual spat on methods resembling those which had been employed in France.

The Emsworth beds, to the north of the entrance of Chichester Harbour, are worked by the Emsworth Dredgermen's Co-operative Society.   They obtained grants from the Board of Trade in order to restrain others from dredging over a limited space.

The South of England Oyster Company (Mr. J. Dilnot, manager), is to the west of the Island.   This company was formed in the year 1865, with a capital of £50,000, in shares of £10 each.   They partially enclosed an area of mud-land in Langston Harbour, about 900 acres in extent, and a smaller area in Chichester Harbour, near the Salterns.   In the first season of the enterprise a " park " was formed on the latter site by laying down 2,000 dozens of hurdles, upon which were placed a quantity of clean coarse ballast, the oysters being laid upon the latter.   The beds are so enclosed, that, by means of sluices, the water could be maintained at any depth, and varied according to the season ; and the quantity of spat preserved in this manner in the breeding seasons of 1866 and 1867 was so great that very sanguine anticipations were formed of the commercial success of the company.

This company also obtained from the Board of Trade a mile in length of deep water within Langston Harbour.   The eastern beds of this company were sold to the Ham and Sea Salter Oyster Company (Mr. W. Gann, manager), in 1880;

since then a large outlay has been expended, and they are now the largest and best-constructed oyster beds in England.

The accompanying Map may assist the reader in following our reference to other buildings and objects in the Island than those already described.

The southern shore of Hayling may be divided into three portions, the western portion being known as Sinah Common and Ballast Bank ; the centre as the South Beach ; and the eastern as the Eastoke Estate and Farm.

Beginning at the extreme west end of this beautiful sea frontage, we find, immediately adjoining the landing place of the ferry from Southsea, a house called the "Round House," and a public-house called " The Norfolk Lodge." Sinah Farm, the land to the eastward of this, comprises about 55 acres, of which 40 are arable and 14 pasture, and has a good farm-house and buildings. Here, also, is the Ballast Bank, which affords an almost unlimited supply of excellent gravel and ballast ; whilst all along the common land on the southern shore there are rabbit warrens, affording abundant sport. Sinah Common comprises about 165 acres, with the sea-frontage of 1 mile and 10 chains ; the South Beach 126 acres and a frontage of 2 miles ; both of these have recently been sold, and sub· divided into plots.

More to the eastward is a pair of four-roomed tenements called "The Lodges."

The terminal station of the Hayling Railway* is within one mile of high-water mark, and is a tasteful and picturesque building of red brick and timber ; but although well arranged, with the necessary waiting rooms, it is somewhat too small even for the present requirements of the traffic, and will require enlargement and reconstruction at an early date.

Near this is a commodious tavern called the " West Town Hotel," erected in a style to harmonize with the station, the estimates for which varied from £845 ! to £2,054 ! !

As we proceed eastward along the beach, the next object is the Life-boat House, a plain but well-constructed brick

---

* This Railway is rented from the Hayling Railway Company, and worked by the London and Brighton Railway Company.

building, which, from the importance of its purpose, demands a special notice. We have mentioned in our historical sketch some vessels which have been wrecked on the coast of this Island, which of course (although fairly sheltered, as we have described it to be, from ordinary bad weather) is exposed to the severity of occasional severe storms.

During the raging of one of these, on the 14th of January, 1865, the ship Ocean, of Plymouth, laden with clay for the manufacture of earthenware, struck upon the bar at the entrance to Langston Harbour. Major Festing, of the Royal Marine Artillery, who resided at Hayling, was at the time stationed in Cumberland Fort, and, seeing the peril of the ship, volunteered to go to its rescue. He was joined by six or eight of the Hayling fishermen, who, on a previous occasion, had saved life from shipwreck in their own boat. On this occasion they went out with Major Festing in a boat belonging to the fort. The sea ran exceedingly high, and more than once the boat, with its gallant crew, was nearly lost; but at length they succeeded in saving the lives of three of the crew, two others having perished. The vessel became a total wreck.

The heroism of Major Festing and his companions excited much interest; and the disaster having attracted the attention of William Leaf, Esq., of Old Change, London, that gentleman presented to the National Life-boat Institution the cost of the Hayling Life-boat, which was shortly afterwards launched under the appropriate name of the "Olive Leaf." Medals were presented to Major Festing and the fishermen for their bravery, and a subscription for the men was raised in Hayling, Havant and Portsmouth. The life-boat house was erected at a cost of £500, to which the late Mr. Sandeman, Sir F. Sykes, Bart., and others of the resident gentry, contributed largely, and the launch of the life-boat was made the occasion of a festive day at Hayling. The Bishop of Chichester attended, and invoked a blessing on the future labours of the "Olive Leaf."

On several occasions since, the life-boat has been useful in saving life.

In 1865 the barque Atlas was wrecked, from which were saved 14 lives.

In February, 1865, 18 lives were saved from the wreck of the barque Lady Westmoreland of Newcastle.

In October, 1870, the brig Lisbon and her crew of seven lives were saved by aid of the life-boat. The boat is carefully protected, and launched for practice once in every three months, under the guidance of Stephen Goldring, the coxswain of the boat, at whose abode, "The Olive Leaf" public-house, a key of the life-boat house is kept. Keys are also available at the Coastguard Station; John Goldring, the assistant coxswain; and at Mr. H. R. Trigg's, the local secretary of the Royal Life-boat Institution.

The next conspicuous building on the beach is a scarcely larger, but far more agreeable object, from a classical design, with a neat Ionic portico and pediment on the north front. This was originally intended for a library, but after remaining unoccupied for many years, it was purchased in the year 1867 by G. R. Divett, Esq., who enlarged the building, added a conservatory on the south side, and made such alterations and repairs as have converted it into a most delightful summer residence, so far as its limited size will permit.

North of the above is the unfinished terrace, known as The Crescent, commenced in 1825; the principal dwelling-house in this row is known as Norfolk House, and is now owned by Dr. How.*

Near this is the Royal Hotel, one of the most essential and agreeable features of Hayling Island. To enlarge upon the importance of a good hotel at a sea-side watering place, is obviously superfluous. The Royal Hotel has now been erected upwards of 66 years, its necessity being even then apparent to some sagacious mind. It is a plain but pleasing structure, shown in the annexed illustration.

There is a pretty croquet ground attached to the building. A billiard room, a spacious public dining room, and twelve

---

* The houses in this terrace have been known at different times, as appears from the catalogues of the auction sales, by the various names of the Esplanade, Padwick Terrace, and Norfolk Crescent. "No. 1, Padwick Terrace, Hayling Beach," was known in 1864 as "Surrey House," and was then occupied by the late Mr. Padwick.

new bed rooms, are amongst the recent additions. There is a convenient coffee room, the whole establishment is replete with every convenience and comfort, and as the Visitors' Book will suffice to prove, it is supported by many members of the higher grades of society. The stabling is excellent in its character, close and open carriages are kept for hire, and under the management the cuisine, wines, and all other details of hotel management, are of the best description, and receive the most careful and constant attention of the experienced conductor of the establishment.*

At the rear of the hotel is a row of cottages and shops.

Not far from the hotel is a building devoted to bathing purposes. It contains hot and cold sea-water baths of the most approved description. For bathing in the sea Mr. Brooks provided 20 commodious and comfortably fitted machines, in each of which is a life-buoy, and these bathing machines were furnished with foot-warmers containing hot water for the use of those who suffer from a chill to the feet after bathing.

In addition to the bathing machines, there was a large floating stage or raft a short distance from the shore, for the use of divers who prefer a plunge without using the machines; this has been removed by the present owner.

Of the excellence of the bathing from the shore at Hayling, we have already spoken, and can only repeat that it cannot be surpassed at any watering place in England.

At the rear of the hotel is the Post Office, which is also a Money Order and Telegraph Station, the postmistress being Miss Jenman. Letters from London are delivered daily in Hayling at 9.0 a.m. and 3.0 p.m. Letters for London are despatched at 10.0 a.m. and 6.0 p.m. The same hours regulate the delivery and despatch of letters from and to Portsmouth, Havant, Chichester, and neighbouring towns.

The telegraph wires were put up in 1872, and messages to and from all parts of the United Kingdom and foreign

* The Royal Hotel was refurnished in 1866 by Messrs. Trollope & Sons, of London, at the cost of Mr. Fuller. A prosperous and well-attended Court of the Ancient Order of Foresters is held at the hotel.

countries are received and transmitted for the Hayling Post Office. The line of telegraph of the Brighton Railway Company, which communicates direct from the Hayling Railway Station to the London Bridge Station, and to Brighton, Hastings, and all other stations of the company, is likewise available to the public for the transmission of messages.

There is also another Post Office near the West Town Hotel. Letter-boxes are erected in many convenient positions on the Island.

Having reached the Bath House, the central point of the sea-frontage of the Island, we may permit the eye to rest upon the beautiful turf, which, above the sand and shingle of the beach, extends from east to west for miles, and forms one of the most attractive features of the place. If it be remembered that on this turf the course was formed on which races were run in 1867, the beauty of the spot and its adaptability for equestrian exercise will at once be recognised.

Towering above the unpretending building referred to, and occupying a commanding position facing the sea, stands West-field House, a beautiful Italian villa, erected in the year 1860 by Mr. H. R. Trigg, South Hayling, from the designs of Mr. A. Trimen, Architect, for the residence of the late G. G. Sandeman, Esq. The house is almost palatial in style and dimension, and has a tasteful turret or belvedere, which commands extensive views in every direction. The house has a magnificent conservatory and excellent domestic offices attached to it. It is surrounded by pleasure grounds and flower and kitchen gardens, about 30 acres, the property is a great ornament to the locality.

Further to the eastward we reach the cottages occupied by the officers and men of the Coastguard Service. There are other Coastguard Stations at Langston Bridge and in Langston Harbour; the men at Hayling being under the superintendence of Mr. C. Dunnoway, chief officer.

Eastoke terminates the sea-frontage of the Island, and brings us to Chichester Harbour, with the beds of the Oyster Company and the Salterns already mentioned. The farm at Eastoke occupies about 311 acres, and is occupied by Mr. H. R. Trigg.

There is a substantial house here, recently erected by Lynch White, of Leigham House, Streatham, Surrey, the present owner of the property. At the entrance to Eastoke are several houses recently erected upon land sold from the estate; other plots are marked out for sale. The views from here of Portsmouth, the Isle of Wight, Selsea Bill, Chichester, Portsdown Hills, and other places, are the most commanding on the Island.

Near the Railway Station are the Gas Works, which were opened by Sir William Humphrey in August, 1877, the first burner being lit by him in the Officers' tent of the Volunteer Camp; the several tents, canteen, kitchen, &c., were fitted up by Mr. H. R. Trigg, through whose energy the Gas Works were principally established.

Immediately after the grant had been obtained from the Rural Sanitary Authority to open up the roads for laying the pipes for the above work, two other companies were registered, one called the Hayling Island Gas Company, and the other the South Hayling Gas and Coal Company; neither of these companies floated, the works are now the private property of Mr. H. R. Trigg. Not far from here is the West Town Post Office; it is a receiving house in connection with the one near the Royal Hotel.

The 1st Administrative Battalion of Hants Volunteers encamped for a fortnight at Hayling, in the month of August or September, from 1872 until 1877.

In former years Witchcraft was much resorted to on the Island. About 75 years ago one Charles Crasweller, an invalid child, was passed through an ash tree, which had previously been split open so far as to allow his body to be passed through, the belief being that if the tree grew together and lived, so would the child recover its strength and live. It is singular they both did so. I have seen both the tree and the man. Before commencing my historical events of Hayling Island, I need only add some general remarks on its social arrangements and other kindred matter.

SPORTS.—Hayling offers many advantages to the lover of Field Sports. The Havant Harriers frequently meet on the

Island; the Hambledon Foxhounds meet in the immediate neighbourhood of Havant, in April and May; there are first-class Steeplechases at Waterloo; the Farlington Racecourse is close to Havant, and Goodwood is easy of access. Races were formerly run on the South Beach, under the patronage of Lord Poulett.

SHOOTING.—In the winter there is some capital wild-fowl shooting round the shores, the widgeon, duck and geese being in abundance this season; five dozen and seven oxbirds were killed from a shoulder gun at one shot. Many men gain their winter livelihood by the use of their punt gun. Partridges and pheasants are plentiful, and rabbits abound. The birds to be found here are the jackdaw, jay, magpie, cuckoo, wryneck, woodpecker, nuthatch, creeper, pheasant, partridge, quail, sand grouse 1890, Montagu harrier 1887, pigeon, ring dove, turtle dove, starling, water ouzle 1835, mistle thrush, fieldfare, redwing, song thrush, blackbird, ring ouzle, Bohemian chatterer, crossbill, bullfinch, bunting, yellow hammer, reed sparrow, house sparrow, kite, buzzard, kestrel, blue hawk, sparrow hawk, white and brown owls, crow, hooded crow, rook (there are two rookeries on the Island, one at the Manor Farm and one at Westfield), land rail, water rail, moorhen, coot, greeb, guillemot, common gull, great grey gull, oyster catcher, dotterel, wild swan, tame swan, bergander, grey goose, bran goose, widgeon, plover, wild duck, teal, sea swallow, snipe, stork, heron, curlew, wombrel, woodcock, peewit, piper, oxbird, titmouse, swallow, marten, swift, night hawk, chaffinch, goldfinch, linnet, sky and tit lark, wagtail, nightingale sparrow, whitethroat, wheatear, black cap, red start, red breast, wren, titmouse, &c.

YACHTING.—Few places can be found so convenient to the yachtsman. Being so close to Cowes, the Royal Yacht Squadron, the Cowes, Ryde, and Portsmouth Yacht Clubs render it one of the best possible residences for yachting purposes. Langston Harbour affords excellent winter mooring ground.

REGATTAS AND BOATING.—Few places can rival with Hayling as regards the extended course that can be obtained, the whole of which would be in view from the beach.   Several regattas were highly commended by the London papers. Boats of all sizes and class can be hired on the beach and in Langston Harbour.   On the beach there are experienced boatmen, who, with their boats, can be hired by the hour.

FISHING.—Excellent sport can be found in both Chichester and Langston Harbours, also in the bay near the rocks.   All the necessary hooks, lines, baits and boats can be had from those plying for hire on the beach or at Langston Harbour.

Amongst the many fish caught in the bay and the sea round the Island are skate, thornback, sting ray, lump fish, eel, conger eel, whiting, plaice, flounders, dab, soles, bream, bass, smelt, mullet, red mullet, mackerel, salmon trout, herring, sprats, cod, dog fish, sand eel, gour fish, lobster, crab, oyster, mussel, cockle, &c.

REPTILES are not numerous on the Island, chief amongst them being the toad, frog, lizard, newt, snake, blind or slow-worm.

The Naturalist will find an inexhaustible charm from the collection he may make at Hayling.

GOLF.—This fascinating game, both to the old and young, seems a pioneer of civilisation over our Common and round about our sand hills.   No wonder the golfer likes Hayling, for here he finds a peaceful spot for health and exercise. The Golf Club has upwards of 180 members; they have erected a pavilion close to their starting point.   Scarcely a day passes without some of its members visiting Hayling.   The links, 18 holes in number, are amongst the best kept in the country, and may well be called the "St. Andrew's of the South."

CRICKET.—Formerly there was a good club; for lack of members it fell.   The same may be said of the Football Club. Both had excellent ground, and some good games have been played.   There are substantial clubs at Havant.

HORTICULTURAL SOCIETY.—This society hold their annual show in August.   It is well supported.   The entries are numerous, and exhibits for flowers, fruit and vegetables above the average merit. It is well conducted, under the excellent management of Mr. E. C. Dowley the hon. sec. The climate is peculiarly adapted to the growth of fruits and flowers, which attain a perfection truly astonishing. I will here give a list of a few wild plants which are found in profusion in our fields and hedgerows :—Common speedwell, yellow iris, common gronswell, comfrey, primrose, cowslip, scarlet pimpernel, henbane, deadly nightshade, sea beat, sea holly, hemlock, parsley, fennels, wild celery, thrift, sea lavender, yellow horned poppy, red poppy, wild or sea spinach, seakale, asparagus, columbine, wood-anemone, common mint, ground ivy, nettle, marjoram, foxglove, water-cress, water-lily, thistles, dandelion, colt's-foot, cuckoo-pent, butcher's-broom.

The annual autumn holiday, which has become a necessity to the dwellers in large towns, and is in fact a great social institution, yearly increases the demand for fresh outlets from London. The extension of the old and the formation of new watering places amply attest this fact. Eastbourne, Littlehampton, Worthing and Bognor are all rising in importance; but not one of these, nor even Brighton itself, possesses natural attractions which can at all compare with those of Hayling.

Almost within the memory of living man Brighton (or Brighthelmstone) was a small, insignificant, and unsightly fishing village. It is represented in engravings executed only sixty years ago as having but a few miserable houses, sufficient for the accommodation of barely a couple of hundred inhabitants; the slopes of the hills, which are now covered with houses, grew corn down almost to the beach, and their summits were crowned with windmills. Patronised, as a residence, by George III., and to a greater extent by his successor, it became a fashionable resort, and the construction of the railway, which places it in direct communication with the metropolis, has led to a growth so rapid and extensive as to be unprecedented.

Bearing these facts in mind, together with the many advantages of Hayling which we have enumerated—especially that its beach is finer than that of Brighton, its facilities for bathing superior, its sea-frontage a mile longer, its roads and rural attractions unequalled elsewhere, and, moreover, that the local rates are less than one-third the amount of those at Portsmouth and Southsea—it is impossible to doubt that the judicious expenditure of capital in building operations is alone requisite to ensure a result resembling that at Brighton in the prosperous future of Hayling Island—

> Where all combined a story tells
> Of simple pleasure, calm delight,
> Of pleasant days and peaceful nights.

In conclusion of my necessarily imperfect description of Hayling, I take the liberty of adding Clement W. Scott, Esq.'s graphic description of the Deserted Island (of Hayling):—

"I have found at last an ideal watering place; the beauty and romance of the Hayling Lanes, with their cottages and trees, are only equalled by the freedom and expanse of the beach, a wild common of furze, a broad parade of green turf calling to the children to use it for cricket, rounders, and romp, a long row of seats facing the water, suggestive of idle mornings and latest novels. Sands to the right and sands to the left, broad expanse of delightful sands, scattered over with shells and seaweeds, provided with bathing machines elaborately made and fitted with polished deal, provided also with life-preservers and hot-water foot baths, according to the fashion of Trouville and Dieppe."

CHAPTER II.

Historical Account of Hayling Island from A.D. 141 *to A.D.* 1891.

BOTH the early and the recent history of Hayling Island are replete with circumstances sufficiently interesting, if not romantic, to deserve narrating at some length.

The whole of the eastern coast of Hampshire was originally peopled by the Belgæ, a Germanic tribe, who landed and settled on the southern coast of Britain at some indefinite period anterior to the Roman invasion. The reason of this choice was probably the facilities afforded for the pursuits of hunting and fishing, and contiguity to the sea. Upon the establishment of the Roman Empire, Chichester, under the name of Regnum, became a military station of importance, and there is reason to believe that a place called Tourner Bury, in the south-eastern part of the Island, may have been a Roman encampment. This occupies a rising ground forming almost a circular vallum; the diameter of its greatest width is 250 yards, and of its narrowest 200 yards; it is surrounded by a fosse which could easily have been filled with water from Chichester Harbour. The vallum is about six feet high, and the fosse was originally of the same depth; but time has lessened the depth of the latter, the banks having washed into it and partially filled it up with leaves and decayed vegetable matter. The interior space contains about three acres, and the furrows across it show that it was at one time under cultivation; there is timber upon it of recent growth, and upon the sides of the vallum are several oak and yew trees, perhaps coeval with the formation of the embankment. No traces of any building, no bones or fragments of any kind to testify its purpose, have, however, yet been found within this space to show its origin or appropriation.

Traces of a Roman road have been discovered leading from Tourner Bury for a distance of several hundred yards in an easterly direction.

A.D. 141. Whilst writing this Second Edition, a more convincing proof of the statement made in my First Chapter referring to the presumed Roman villa cannot be found than in the fact of the owner of the property having just (1892) found on the site of the recent excavation a coin, in good preservation, of " Faustina," the daughter of Annius Versus, a prefect of Rome; she married Antonius Pius, and died in the third year of her husband's reign, 36 years of age. Antonius Pius was born A.D. 86. He became Emperor on the death of Adrian, A.D. 138 and died A.D. 161. Part of a temple erected to Antonius and Faustina still exists in the Campo Vaccino of Rome. His conquests in Britain are confirmed by Lollius Urbicus. Possibly the villa referred to might have been the residence of Antonius whilst in England. He inherited great wealth and had a taste for country life.

The Saxons are known to have landed at Christchurch and Portchester, both on the Hampshire coast, and also at West Wittering, which immediately adjoins Hayling on the east; and a Saxon leader named Ella is supposed to have disembarked there, the precise place of his landing being known by the name of Ellanore.

1045. The earliest record of Hayling refers to the year 1045, when the manor was presented by Emma, the mother of Edward the Confessor, to the Church of Winchester and the monks there serving God. Queen Emma had been twice married, first to Ethelred the Unready, and afterwards to Canute. How she became possessed of Hayling does not appear, but the circumstances which led her to endow the religious establishment at Winchester with this manor are extremely curious. It appears that Edward the Confessor was induced by Godwin Earl of Kent, and Robert Archbishop of Canterbury, to accuse his mother of endeavouring to prevent his accession to the throne, of consenting to the murder of her younger son Alfred, and of criminal intimacy with Alwin, Bishop of Winchester. Emma, through the bishops, who were faithful to her interests, demanded a public trial by the ordeal of hot iron. This ordeal consisted in the accused person walking, with bare feet, upon a number of red-hot ploughshares, and during many centuries it was frequently employed as a test of guilt or innocence. The queen underwent this ordeal in Winchester Cathedral, in presence of the Confessor, with a number of bishops and nobles. We are told that she saw St. Swithin, to whom the church was dedicated, in a vision, and that the Saint promised her immunity from the ordeal on condition that she forgave her son his accusation of her. Appealing to heaven for deliverance, the queen pressed upon nine red-hot plough-shares with the whole weight of her body, without feeling any heat. This was of course regarded as a miracle, and the king melted to tears of contrition, prostrated himself before his mother and entreated her forgiveness. In gratitude for the supposed intervention of Providence, the monks of Winchester became enriched with the gift of twenty-one manors, three of which were bestowed upon them by the King, nine others, including " Haylynge," by Queen Emma, and nine by Bishop Alwyn, who had been implicated with her. The Queen died in 1052, and was buried in the church at Winchester. This incident is copiously and dramatically described in a mediæval manuscript, entitled *Annales Ecclesiæ Wintoniensis*, quoted in Wharton's *Anglia Sacra*.

1066. William the Conqueror granted a church at Hayling to the Abbey Church of the Blessed Mary and St. Peter of Jumièges, Normandy, and Henry II., who died in 1189, confirmed this grant. The date of the submerged church may possibly be about 1045, of which alone the font remains, now fixed upon a pedestal near the pulpit in St. Mary's church, South Hayling.*

1080. It is interesting, also, to notice in the Domesday Survey references to the saltern and the fisheries still existing on the Island.

* As neither St. Peter's, North Hayling, nor St. Mary's, South Hayling, were built until after 1272, it cannot refer to either of these.

The next reference to Hayling is the following passage in
" Domesday Book " :—

1080. " Hantescire. The land of the King. In Boseberg
Hundred. The King himself holds in Hantescire. The land
of St. Peter of Jumièges. In Boseberg Hundred. The
Abbey of Jumièges holds Helinghey.* Alward held it allodi-
ally of Queen Eddid (Emma). It was then taxed for twelve
hides,† now for seven hides ; the land is fourteen carucates.
There are in demesne two carucates, and twenty-three villains,
and twenty-seven borderers, with seventeen ploughs. There
are three servants and a saltern of the value of six shillings
and eight pence, and two fisheries of twenty pence, and one
acre of meadow. There is wood for the pannage of twenty
hogs. In the time of King Edward it was worth fifteen
pounds, and afterwards ten pounds, now twelve pounds, and
yet it renders fifteen pounds at farm. The monks of the
bishoprick of Winchester claim this manor, because Queen
Imma (Emma) gave the same to the Church of St. Peter and
St. Swythun, and then put the monks in possession of a
moiety. The other moiety she demised to Ulward for his life,
only so that after his death and burial the manor should
revert to the monastry. And so Ulward held part of the
manor of the monks until he died, in time of King William.
This is so attested by Elsi, Abbott of Ramsey, and by the
whole hundred."

The Abbot Elsi here mentioned was appointed to that
dignity in 1080, and held it for eight years.

The above passages are interesting and important in several
ways. They evidently refer to three different properties into
which the Island had been divided. The first and smallest
of these, viz., Eaststoke Manor, belonging to the Conqueror,

---

* Hayling is sometimes spelt *Harenge* in the early records. In Domesday it is spelt *Halingei, Helinghei,* and *Helingey.* The word is supposed
to be derived from the Saxon *healle inge* and *ey,* signifying the place of the
meadow in which there was an *aula,* or hall, answering to the modern
hall or *mansion* ; or, as all islands were in early times considered objects
of sanctity, the name may have been derived from the Saxon *helige,* which
signified *holy* or *sacred.*

† The hide of land may be roughly taken at 100 acres.

by right of conquest, had previously been seized by Harold; the second refers to land, which would appear from other sources to have been granted to the monks of Winchester by King Ethelred; whilst the third and much the larger of the three is that given by Queen Emma to the monks of Winchester. This, there is every reason to suppose, had been seized by William the Conqueror and given by him to the Abbey of Jumièges in Normandy.*

This once famous abbey enshrined the remains of the Conqueror's mother, and was endowed by him with other English possessions besides Hayling. Its towers are still to be seen looming upon the horizon in the centre of a peninsula formed by the windings of the river Seine. They are in ruins, but of exceeding beauty, and attest the grandeur and magnificence of the house when in its zenith. Its immediate possessions originally extended on the right bank of the Seine from Duclair to Caudebec, but were subsequently limited to a space of twelve miles in circumference. The extensive site occupied by this monastery and its appendages ceases to be a matter of surprise when we learn that before the death of the first abbot there were at Jumièges 900 monks and 1,500 lay brethren as inmates of the monastery.

1086. Again referring to " Domesday Book," we read :—

" Hantescire. The land of the King in Boseberg Hundred. The King holds in Halingei two hides and a half. Leman held it of King Edward in parage. Harold took it from him when he seized upon the Kingdom, and put it into his farm, and it is yet there. It was then assessed at two hides and a half; now for nothing. In demesne there is one carucate; and one villain and eight borderers, with half a carucate and one acre and a half of meadow. In the time of King Edward it was worth 40s., and afterwards 20s., now 70s.

" Hantescire. The Abbey of St. Peter of Winchester. In Boseberg Hundred. The monks of the bishopric of Winchester

---

* The Abbey of Jumièges is situated in the Pays de Caux, upon the river Seine, five leagues above Rouen, the capital of Upper Normandy. It was founded by St. Philibert A.D. 650; he was the first abbot for the reception of Benedictine monks under the reign of Clovis II. who, with St. Batilda his wife, were the principal benefactors.

4

hold,Helinghei. They always held it. In the time of King Edward it was taxed at five hides, and now for four hides; the land is two carucates. There are eleven villains with three carucates and a half, and one acre of meadow. In the time of King Edward it was worth 100s., and afterwards £4; now it is worth £4 10s."

1100. Reverting to that portion of the Hayling lands alluded to in the Domesday Book* as belonging to the Abbey of Jumièges, we find that very soon after the first grant by William I. it was confirmed by Henry I. between 1100 and 1109, as follows: "Henry King of England to Anselm Archbishop of Canterbury, William Bishop of Winchester, Henry de Port Sheriff, and other his faithful men, French and English, of Hampshire, greeting: Know ye, that I grant to St. Peter of Jumièges, Haringey, and all things that pertain to it, with sac and soc, and thol and theam, and infangenethef, with all other customs, nor will I suffer that any one take or diminish anything therefrom. Witness, Robert Earl of Medelent, &c., at Winchester."

1155. Henry II., who ascended the throne in 1155, further confirmed this gift "to the church of the Blessed Mary and St. Peter of Jumièges, and the monks there serving God"— "to wit, of the gift of King William in England, the greater part of the Island of Haringey, with the church and tithes of the whole Island, except the tithes of pulse and oats in the land of the Bishop of Winchester, and, in the same Island, sac and soc, and thol and theam, and infangenethef, with all other customs." This charter was witnessed by Rotrold Archbishop of Rouen, and is dated from Rouen.

The grant of *thol* in these charters was the privilege to buy and sell, or keeping a market, and it meant also the customary dues paid to the lord for his profits of a fair or market, as well as a tribute or custom for passage (Bract. lib. ii., cap. 24, s. 3); and under these charters the ferries at the eastern and western harbours, and the passage-money paid to the ferrymen, passed to the Abbey of Jumièges.

---

* Domesday Book was completed in the twentieth year of William, A.D. 1086.

1216. When the valuable record known as the *Testa de Nevill* was compiled—in the latter part of the reign of Henry III., and the commencement of that of Edward I.—we find that certain land of the King in the Island of Hayling was held by the then Earl of Arundel; and that four hides of land of ancient feoffment in this Island were held of the said Earl by the Prior of Rungeton or Runcton, a manor in Sussex.

1241. In the early part of the reign of Henry III., and certainly previous to the year 1241, a priory was built in the Island in order that the services of the church might be duly performed, and the revenues of the manor collected with regularity; and we are told by Deshayes, in his *Histoire de l'Abbaye Royale de Jumièges*, that the priory founded by the monks in the "Isle of Helling" returned them an annual income of eleven hundred golden crowns.

The prior was appointed by and dependent on the foreign house, and was removable at pleasure. On one occasion when aid was granted to the King, the Prior of Hayling was summoned, and pleaded that the priory was alien and not conventual, and that all the priors of the same, from time whereof the memory of man ran not to the contrary, had been appointed and removed at the motion and will of the Abbot of St. Peter of Jumièges, in Normandy, and were not perpetual and not inducted.

Of the priory itself no remains are at the present day to be found, but it has been conjectured that it was near the place called Tourner Bury, already mentioned. Among the closes in this neighbourhood are some called Chappel Park, Monks' Land, and Abbot's Land, and dressed stones, with mortar adhering to them, are said to have been ploughed up in the locality. This, however, must have been after the submergence of the first church at Hayling, to which we shall presently have occasion to allude.

1241. From the *Notitia Monastica* we learn that the Priory of Hayling was a cell to the foreign Benedictine abbey, and it is interesting to read the rules of the monastic order, and to allow the imagination to wander back to the time when the beautiful paths and meadows of the Island were traversed by holy men in cowl, tunic, and scapula, made of the cheapest stuff the country afforded; whose beds were a mat, a straw pallet, a piece of serge, a blanket, and a pillow, and whose meals were limited to two different dishes at dinner, with fruit, three quarters of a pint of wine per day, and one pound of bread a day for both dinner and supper.

At the date of the *Testa de Nevill* the Prior held his lands in Helinge "in pure alms of the lord the king-in-chief."

Subsequently a serious dispute arose between the Prior and the Vicar of Hayling, the latter claiming the tithes of the parish as belonging to his church, whilst the prior claimed them as given to the Norman Abbey by William the Conqueror. The vicar (Master Nicholas de Rye) went so far as to excommunicate the prior, who was his religious superior. In Michaelmas Term, 1241, the prior sued the vicar at Westminster for these tithes, and laid his damages at £100. The vicar was prohibited from prosecution, and ordered to absolve the prior from excommunication; but refusing compliance, he was put under restraint, and eventually withdrew his claim to a greater amount of tithe than his predecessor had enjoyed. He also absolved the excommunication, and confirmed his submission by a deed delivered to the prior.

1253. Another knotty question at this period of our history was the right of free warren, which was highly valued. This was a privilege to the lord, exclusive of all other persons, to keep and to take birds of game and animals of chase. In the time of the Conqueror the penalty upon offenders sporting in a warren was loss of eyes, or mutilation; and 300 years later (in 1471) the Bishop of Chester issued a mandate to one of his deans to the effect that "certain persons, sons of damnation, seduced by the spirit of the devil, and laying aside the fear of God," having broken into his park at Selsey, and chased, killed, and carried away the deer and other wild beasts, such persons were "adjudged to have incurred the penalty of excommunication by bell, book, and candle."*

---

* The form of excommunication is given by Sterne in "Tristram Shandy," both in Latin and English, from the records of Rochester Cathedral; and another, almost precisely similar, may be found in Spelman's Glossary, p. 205. The awful language of imprecation and cursing hurled upon the soul, body, limbs, and "every portion of the

1253. So difficult, however, was the tithe controversy that it led to the intervention of Pope Innocent, who, by a bull addressed in 1253 to the Dean and Warders of the Friars Minor at Winchester, referred the settlement of the question to them. Their proceedings in the matter, including a taxation of the vicarage, which they made " with the counsel of prudent men," are on record, and from these it appears that the Abbey of Jumièges was legally possessed of two-thirds of all the tithes in Hayling and the right of patronage, under their original charter from the Conqueror, and that the remaining third part, then in possession of Nicholas de Rye, who had been instituted by the Bishop of Winchester, had also been granted to the Abbey of Jumièges, in reversion, on his decease. This portion probably consisted of the tithes of pulse and oats excepted in the charter of Henry II., which the Popes had wrested from the Bishops of Winchester. This being so, upon the death of Nicholas de Rye they would become entitled to the tithes, great and small, of the whole Island ; and out of this, therefore, the vicarage was carved under the taxation above referred to. The litigation involved some curious points of ecclesiastic practice, as between the pope, the bishops, and the clergy of the period, into which our space will not permit us to enter.

1266. A subsequent Earl of Arundel founded an abbey at Troarn, in the Diocese of Bayeux, in Normandy ; and in 1266 the abbot of that monastery granted all the lands he held in the Island of " Heling " to John Fauconer de la Wade, to hold the same in peace for ever, doing the chief lords of the fee the accustomed service.

In the same year Henry III. granted to the same De la Wade free warren in all his lands in the Island, but without words of perpetuity ; and to William, another member of the family, the wreck of the sea in the Hundred of Boseberg, as well within as without the Isle of Hayling.

1272. There are still extant some accounts of the reeve or bailiff of the manor, kept at the same early period to which

members " of the luckless offender, in the name of the Holy Trinity, angels, archangels, prophets, martyrs, and saints, might well induce Uncle Toby to exclaim, " Our Armies swore terribly at Flanders, but nothing to this. For my own part, I could not have a heart to curse my dog so."

we have referred (the reign of Edward I.). These contain much curious information as to the prices of provisions, labour and materials; and the following account of the issues of the Grange, taken in conjunction with the large amounts claimed in the legal proceedings above mentioned, show that the Island must have been a place of considerable importance, and its agricultural produce large. The stock upon the manor consisted of 3 cart-horses, 4 bullocks, 2 pack-horses, 2 colts, 18 oxen, 11 steers, 11 calves, 1 bull, 29 cows, 16 heifers, 4 hides, 244 muttons, 95 two-year old sheep, 97 lambs, 116 ewes, 53 hogs, 331 wool pelts, "sent to Ramsey, 4 pea-hens, 80 geese, 20 capons, 28 hens, a hive of bees, 200 hens' eggs, 280 cheeses, 30 gallons of butter, 192 doves out of the dovecote, and 2 lbs. of honey."

1272 to 1461. We now come to what is undoubtedly the most important event in the history of the Island— namely, a great inundation, or rather a series of inundations of the sea, whereby a very considerable area of land was irrecoverably submerged. From the reign of Edward I. to that of Edward IV. (a period of 275 years) this portion of the southern coast was subject to serious inroads of the ocean, with very disastrous consequences. The whole coast, as far eastward as Hastings, suffered severely from this cause, and the public records of the period contain numerous proofs of the mischief that was done by the water.

The fact of this submergence of a portion of Hayling Island rests upon documentary evidence of unquestionable authority, but it is extremely difficult, at this distant period, to define with anything like accuracy the extent of the surface covered by the sea. The measurements of area given in the old records are so various and uncertain, and the changes of ownership from time to time so puzzling, that no correct estimate on this point can be arrived at.

In 1279 the Abbot of Jumièges was summoned to answer the King before the justices-itinerant at Winchester, by what warrant (*quo warranto*) he claimed free warren in all his demesne lands in Hayling without the will of the King and his predecessors, but by the verdict of the knights summoned to try the issue the abbot was confirmed in this right.

1285. The existence of slavery* in England is a fact which it is hard to realise; but there is something very like it in the annals of Hayling Island. There is no doubt that before the Norman Conquest serfdom was a common condition with many, and subsequently it appears that there were " villains regardant," or attached to the manor or land, and " villains in gross," or annexed to the person of the lord, and transferable from one owner to another. The latter the lord had power to rob and chastise as he pleased, provided he did not maim them. And we find that in 1285 (13 Edward I.), Alice, the wife of Thomas le Clerk, claimed before the court of the Abbot of Jumièges that a false judgment had been pronounced against her in the same court. At the hearing Henry le Palmer claimed that he had bought certain tenements of the lord as his villanage, and that Maud, the mother of the plaintiff Alice, had been *sold* out of the manor as a villain, and that the custom of the manor would not allow any male or female villain sold out of the manor to return and claim their rights. The jury found that the defendant had the greater right to the premises, and judgment went in his favour as the villain of the prior; Alice and her husband being remitted to make their demand against the prior, if it seemed to them expedient.

1292. In the valuation of Pope Nicholas, made in the 20th Edward I., 1292, we have the following entries of rating:—

The Church of Heylingg . . £80 0 0 £8 0 0
The Vicarage of the same . . . £14 6 8 £1 6 8

1293. In the return of the value of Hayling Priory and its possession in England.

The reeve's account stated that the prior held a manor and a garden, with a dove-house within the close, worth 50s. a year; three hundred and sixty-six acres of waste land in demesne, worth by the year £12 4s. 2d., ten acres of wood, worth by the year 20s.; one hundred acres of pasture land for sheep, 16s. 8d.; one water mill, worth by the year 60s.; sum of the

---

* Amongst our Saxon ancestors there appears to have been two species of slaves, the survus or household slave, and the villien præcdal or rustic slave, who attended to the concerns of agriculture alone.

whole, £19 10s. 10d. There were forty-eight customary tenants holding forty virgates and a half of land, worth £24 2s. 5d. at the term of Saint Thomas the Apostle, their works being of the value of £16 16s. 9¼d., Nicholas de Leigh and William Coleman paying 15d. and five capons of the value of 10d., at the feast of Saint Michael; foreign rents at Portsmouth, 76s. 2d., that he held the church to his own proper use, £80—the whole manor, including the church, being valued at the sum of £144 8s. 3½d. Amongst the utensils and goods of the Abbey at Hayling are enumerated: One palfrey, price 60s.; one sumpter horse, 40s.; two asses, price 4s.; also seven score of ewes in the town of Estling (Eastoke), in the custody of Adam Browne, are worth 112s. 8d.; in the granary five quarters of barley for the household, 20s.; two quarters of old peas to be distributed in alms; the crops of one hundred and ten acres of corn, £19 6s. 9d.; eighty-six acres of barley, £8 12s.; eleven and a half acres of oats, 17s. 3d.; eighty acres of peas, £4; and the crop of seventy-eight and a half acres of peas, £78 6s.; the value of the articles enumerated being £67 16s., the tithes being in addition.

1294. In the year 1294, Edward I. seized upon all the alien priories in this country which were dependent upon Norman abbeys; and not only was the Abbot of Jumièges deprived of his cell at Hayling, with all its possessions, but the unfortunate head of that establishment was seized into the hands of the King. The warrant is still in existence under which Simon de Marsham was assigned to seize and safely keep the priory and all its possessions, together with the prior himself, and to return an inventory of the effects so seized to the Barons of the Exchequer.

The return to this writ is also extant, and we there find that the possessions of the priory comprised a manor and garden, 110 acres of corn, 86 acres of barley, 11½ acres of oats, 80 acres of peas, 100 acres of pasture, 10 acres of wood, and 366 acres of waste land in demesne, together with one water-mill. It also appears that there were 48 customary tenants, holding 40½ virgates of land; the whole manor, including the church, being valued at £144 8s. 3½d. Among the utensils and goods of the abbey are enumerated one palfrey, price 60s.; one sumpter horse, price 4os.; two asses, 4s.; seven score ewes in the town of Estling (Estoke), worth 112s. 8d.; in the granary, 5 quarters of barley for the household, 2os.; 2 quarters of old peas to be distributed in alms, and the crops of the before-mentioned arable land.

1304. (31st Edwd. I.) Either John le Fauconer or his son died, and was found on inquisition to have been seized of five score acres and three hundred acres of land at Hayling.

1315. In the 9th Edwd. II. John le Botiler assumed to be entitled to wreck, and sought to recover for the seizure by others of five tuns of wine at Emsworth—a village opposite the north-east angle of the Island—but failed to substantiate his claim.

Ill-defined and conflicting rights, with consequent litigation, have characterized the recent history of Hayling to an extraordinary degree, and there are many instances of similar disputes in ancient times. Thus in the very year last mentioned John le Botiler and Joan his wife, who had inherited from the Le Fauconers, were attached to answer certain tenants, or "men of the said John and Joan of the Manor of Helinge," because they required other services than those which their ancestors had rendered when the manor was in the hands of the former Kings of England.

The tenants set forth that in the time of William the Conqueror every tenant had been accustomed to hold one messuage and one virgate* of land, by the service of five shillings and eightpence farthing by the year, and that on the death of an ancestor they used to give half a mark—instead of which the defendants now demanded one mark—for entry upon every acre of land. They also complained that the Le Botilers demanded "ransom of flesh and blood, tallaging them

---

* The number of acres in the hide and virgate was not uniform. The hide generally contained 120 acres, *i.e.*, four virgates or yard-lands of 30 acres. At Runwell the hide anciently contained only 80 acres. At Nastok it contained 140. At Sandon the virgate consisted of 60 acres, at Wicham of 24, at Nastok of 20, and at Drayton of 16. The acre consisted as at present of 160 square perches, the perch being 16½ feet.— Archdeacon Hale, in the "Domesday of St. Paul's," Camden Society's Publications, No. LXIX. p. lxiii.

high and low at will, grievously distraining them from day to day." The damages were laid at £1,000 to the King and £500 to the tenants.

Domesday Book was formally put in evidence for the tenants, but the defendants urged that the Abbot of Troarn had enfeoffed John le Fauconer, the ancestor of the female defendant, of the lands, and supported their own view of the services claimed.

At the trial, John de Botiler absented himself. His wife, however, stated her own case, and on a further hearing the tenants in turn absented themselves, and a verdict confirming the services claimed by Joan was recorded

1316. In Parliamentary Writ, 9 Edwd. II. The Prior of Hayling certified to writ, tested A. Chipston 5th March, as lord of the township of North and South Hayling, in the County of Southampton.

1322. One interesting document bearing on the subject of the inundations is a petition presented to the Crown by the Prior of Hayling, in 1324, alleging that the church and a large portion of his lands had been inundated by the sea, submersed, and destroyed.

1324. On March 8th, 1324, a warrant was issued by King Edward to enquire into the damage done by inundations. On the inquisition being held at "Hailyngge," by the before-mentioned keepers of the alien priories, before twelve jurymen, whose names are on record, the said jury found that 206 acres of arable and 20 acres of pasture land *belonging to the Priory* had been destroyed by the sea since the house was first seized by Edward I.; that six virgates of land of the customary tenants had in like manner been submersed and destroyed; that nearly the whole hamlet of Estoke, and a part of the hamlet of Northwood, had also been submersed, and that two mills belonging to the priory were deteriorated 20s. a year by the same cause; and that the annual value of the possessions destroyed by the sea amounted to £42 7s. 4d.—in those days a large sum of money.

By a subsequent charter, the King remitted to the prior a part of the payment which he was bound to make in time of war, on account of the devastation made by the inroads of the sea.

1325. (18th Edward II.) The alien religious houses in Hampshire were in the charge of keepers—Ralph de Bereford and Richard de Westcote—who made a fresh return of the possessions of Hayling Island.

The prior thereupon appeared before the Treasurer and Barons of the Exchequer at Westminster, and earnestly prayed that his house, with its appurtenances, might be committed to him for safe custody. The Crown consented to the petition of the prior, and committed to him the keeping of his house and all the issues thence received, saving to the Crown the prayers of the church and military services when they should happen to be required, and upon condition that all the animals and chattels should be kept in good order and sustenance, and for the safe custody of these the prior had to find security.

1327. Assessment for the subsidy, A.D. 1327, 1st., Edward III. Hayling, in the Hundred of Bosmere:—

Villata de Northwood.—Mathew Sorell, 4s. 2d. ; William le Marche, 6s. 6d. ; Galfridus Segare, 4s. ; William Kerps, 12d. ; John Jordan, 4s. ; Henry Seman, 2s. , Thomas le Croke, 2s. ; Robert le Mone, 19s. ; Thomas de Honore, 3s. 9d. ; Simon le Bastem, 4s. 6d. ; William le Mone, 2s. ; Godfrey le Lapse, 18d. ; Robert Whickers, 13d. ; Richard Kerps, 2s. ; Simon Shude, 7d. ; sma, 40s. 8d.

Villata de Estoke.—William Cauntels, 2s. ; John de Estoke, 2s. 6d. ; Walter Hamond, 7d. ; John le Coke, 4s. 9d. ; sma, 10s. 10d.

Villata de Stokes—Robert Daniel, 5s. ; Thomas Hereberd, 3s. 3d. ; John Curtais, 2s. ; Robert le Hayward, 2s. ; Robert William, 3s. 4d. ; John Juselyr, 3s. ; William le Yonge, 3s. ; Alicia Rebecca William Thomas Widow, 5s. ; sma, 27s. 7d,

Villata de Southwood—Richard Selbat, 18d. ; Thomas Higgeworth, 2s. 6d. ; Nico. Curtays, 6s. ; Thos. Wilkyne, 6s. ; Alicia Rebecca Wm. Le Boys, 3s. 6d. ; Rebecca Calle, 12d. ; Rebecca Selbati, 1s. ; Wm. Mercatore, 14d. ; Henry le Pasteur, 15d. ; Rebecca Gofayre, 12d. ; sma, 25s. 6d.

Villata de Meyngham.—William le Gond, 2s. ; William le Rynere, 15s. 8d. ; Walter le Webbe, 4s. 6d. ; John atte Stubbe, 2s. ; William atte Purye, 2s. 3d. ; William de Walberton, 7s. ; John Seman, 3s. ; Eustace de Meyngham, 2s. 7d. ; Walter

Pegas, 14d.; Recta Ryneld, 4s.; Peter le Webbe, 12d.; sma., 30s.

Villata de Westeton.—John de Westeton, 2s.; Rco. Raggond, 2s.; John Curtays, 12d.; Henry le Haywarde, 12d.; Wm. Bokat, 12d.; John Red, 12d.; John Welkyne, 4s.; Wm. Youngman, 18d.; Rco. Gerard, 2s.; Walter le Suthstone 2s.; Thos. Abbod, 2s.; Henry Atte Hoke, 7s.; Henry Seymoure, 10s.; Richard atte Flute, 12d.; Richard Miles, 7d.; Richard atte Stubbe, 7d.; Wm. le Mareshal, 7d.; sma, 39s. 10d.

1351. Land in Hayling appears to have belonged to the Prior and Convent of de Calceto, or the Causeway, near Arundel, and were held by a second John le Botiler as trustee for them. Through subsequent holders they passed to Sir Thomas Lewknor who was attainted in the reign of Richard III., when his lands at Hayling were escheated to the Crown; and in 1524 the Convent of de Calceto was suppressed under a royal licence by Cardinal Wolsey, on whose disgrace their possessions passed into the hands of the Crown. The subsequent history of the descent of this part of the Island has little of general interest.

Extract from Manor Rolls.

1371. A barrel of soap, which had been cast on shore, of the value of 9s., was seized to the use of the lord.

1377 to **1480.** Remissions of taxation were made by Richard II., Henry IV., and Edward IV. in consequence of further inundations. In one of the petitions it is stated that the place where the parish church was at first built was in the centre of the Island; that within living memory it stood by the sea-shore in good preservation; but that at the date of the petition it was so deep in the sea that an English vessel of the larger class could pass between it and the land, from which it was distant about two miles.*

---

* " Leuca," the word used in the petition, is spoken of by Ingulphus as a mile. Bloomfield, in his *History of Norfolk*, renders "leuca" a league. The ordinary English mile was, in former times, a traditional measure, being, in fact, nearly a mile and a half of the present standard.

1391. Simon Dubosc, Abbot of Jumièges, retired from that place to Hayling, having obtained a restoration of the priory; three monks came with him to re-establish discipline, and they continued to enjoy the revenues of the priory till 1413, when alien priories were for the most part dissolved. Abbot Dubosc was buried at Jumièges, where his monumental effigy, which is an excellent work of art, and obviously a likeness, may still be seen in excellent preservation.

Again from the Estoke Manor Rolls,* we read :—

1396. Also the whole Homage presents that Richard Clere found upon the shore at Crakehorde, a dead man by wreck of the sea upon whom was found certain chattels, and of money in his purse, 3s. 5d.; his clothes, price 1s. 4d. Also upon Henry Mulward in the same manner of money, 3s. 4d.; and of other things valued at 1s. Also on Roger Bohun of money, 18s. 4d.; and of other things valued, and his clothes, 2s. 8d. Also upon John Danell in money, 1od.; and of his clothes valued at 6d. Also upon John Legard of money, 1s. 3d.; and on his clothes, 4d. Also upon Lawrence Bover of money, 16s.; and of his clothes valued at 1s. 8d., and one silver Seal, weight 1s. 8d.; also one Baselard, one Girdle with silver Harness, price†—remaining in the custody of Evyk, servant of Maud Chandler, also two obligations, one made to Thomas Waryn, and the other to Henry Elone of Shoreham, also three letters. Also upon Henry Jurdan, of money, 3s.; and of his clothes valued at 2s. Also upon Lilelman, of money, 1½d.; of his clothes valued at 6d. Also upon Robert Wade, of money, 5d.; and of his clothes valued at 8d. Also upon Margery atte Hasle, of money 4s. 9½d.; and of his clothing valued at 1s. 8d. Also upon William Wade, of money ½d.; and of his clothing valued at 1s. Also upon Roger Palframan, of money, 2s. 4d.; and of his clothing 1s. Also upon Henry Bohun, of money, ½d., and of his clothing 8d., and one dagger with silver harness. Also upon Nicholas Joie,

---

* The Manor Rolls of Northstoke, Eastoke, and Westhay were kindly placed in my hands to take this and other extracts by favour of Lynch White, Esquire, of Leigham House, Streatham, Surrey, the present owner.

† No price is here quoted.

of money, 3s. 4d.; and of his clothes 6s. Also upon Thomas Smith, of money, 9d.; and of his clothing 1s. Also upon John Mulward, of money, 6d.; of his clothing valued at 1s. 4d. Also upon Peter Bedford, of money 9s.; and of his clothing 1s. 4d. (which remain in the custody of T. Bocker, of his liberty, and T. Call). Also upon John Passage, in money 5d.; and of his clothing valued at 6d. Also of certain other chattels, four bags, a packsaddle, six yards of murrain, and two bits; price in the whole 3s. 4d. Also one little boat, price 5s., arising to the lord of wreck of the sea. Also upon two clerks, Walter Day and Thomas Stacey, it is to be required of concerning their gear.

The above entry undoubtedly records the result of some sad shipwreck, in which no less than 21 persons lost their lives, their property, &c., falling into the hands of the lord, the total value of which amounted to 104s. 9d.

In another extract from the same Manor Rolls:—

1398. The Homage present that Amayette Thorn, who held of the lord in widowhood one messuage and 12 acres of bond land in the tithing of Westhay, hath left the lordship and withdrawn herself for felony committed, and so the messuage and lands aforesaid remain in the hands of the lord, and upon which messuage and lands proclamation hath been made according to the custom of the manor, and no one comes to challenge. Therefore let them remain.

In the same year and under the Manor of Northstoke, Richard Parker at this court comes and takes of the lord one messuage and four acres of bond land in Estoke, formerly of Richard Mulward as that which fell into the hands of the lord by escheat because no one of the blood, although proclamation has been made according to the custom of the manor, would fine for the same. To hold to him and his heirs according to the custom by the service therefore, due and before of right accustomed, for which entry he gives to the lord of a fine 3s. 4d., and did fealty.

The value of the Heriotts at this time were: a horse 13s. 4d., a cow, 6s. 8d., an ox, 8s., a wether 1s. 8d.

1407. In Eastoke Manor, the court of the term of St. Martin, holden there on Thursday next after the feast of

Saint Lucy the virgin, in the eighth year of the reign of King Henry. John Cantelow, of the common suit by Thomas Danell. The Homage there present that William Segare, tenant-at-will, hath made default, therefore he is in mercy. Also they present that Joan, the daughter of Walter Parson, hath married one John Wargen (without the licence of the lady) dwelling within the lordship, who gives to the lady for the price of the marriage 1s., according to the custom.

Also they present that two empty pipes, one small chest empty, and one trunk of a tree called toppeley, broken in the whole price 1s. 8d., arising of wreck of the sea upon the land of the lady at Estoke, which was seized by the wrecker of the lady, and delivered for the stock of the lady at Lambourne.

1413. The religious community at Hayling became a priory, subject to the Abbey of Jumièges, and this relationship between the two establishments was maintained until the year 1413, when, with other alien priories, the former was suppressed.

The suppressed priory was granted by Henry V. to the new monastery of Shene (Richmond) in Surrey.

1540. In the Valuation of Shene priory, 32 Henry VIII., anno 1540, County Southampton :—

Hayling Ferma Priorat	. . .	£56	0 0
„ Mol Agnot .	. . .	1	0 0
„ Pergin Cur .	. . .	3	1 11

1541. On the dissolution of monasteries by Henry VIII. the Manor and Rectory of Hayling, as part of the possessions of the religious house of Shene, passed into the hands of the Crown, and in 1541 was granted by Henry to the College of the Holy Trinity at Arundel, in exchange for the Manor of Bury, in the County of Sussex. This college was surrendered to the Crown in 1544, and all its possessions, including Hayling, were then granted by the King to the Earl of Arundel, a grant which was confirmed by Queen Mary in the first year of her reign, and the Earls of Arundel and their successors, the Dukes of Norfolk, continued lords of the manor of Hayling till 1825.

After this period the priory appears to have fallen rapidly into decay, the prior's stables alone being mentioned in the minister's accounts of 32 Henry VIII. (1541).

These successive noblemen resided at Arundel, about twenty miles from Hayling; the courts of the manor were held by their steward, and the demesne lands farmed by their bailiffs, or let; and under their lordships the history of Hayling presents nothing worthy of special record.

1544. The two fisheries of the value of twenty pence, mentioned in the Domesday Survey, were those of the east and west shores of the Island, and in these, from the earliest periods, weirs were fixed for taking the fish with which the harbour has always been abundantly supplied. Rents of 6d. and 12d. per weir were paid to the lord in the time of Edward VI., and there are many similar entries on the court rolls. In 1544 William Pepsham rented, at 10d. a year, a place to build at his own expense a dam called a weir.

1544. Referring to the Assessments, we find in the Subsidy Roll, 37 Henry VIII., there were at Northwood in Hayling, 22 assessments, raising £5 6s. 8d.; in Southwood, 20, raising £8 7s. 8d.; in the latter place, John Pytcombe was assessed for £20, in goods £1 8s.; John Tawke, £20—£1 6s. 8d.; John Kempe, land and fees, £1 8s.; the church scole, £13 13s.

1552. In the Record of Church Goods of the 6th Edward VI., of Hayling, Northwood. The inventory of Goods, Plate, Jewells, Bells, &c., ornaments of the Church of Hayling, taken the 15 day of July, anno sexto Edward sixth. Presented by Richard Pepesham and John Lemay. Items— Plums, Toowe Chalesses of Silver, with a paten, 2 Corporas Clothes, 4 Aulter clothes, 3 Vestments, 2 Coopes, 1 Paule cloth, 2 stremers, 2 baners, 3 Bells in Styple. A payre of Sencers, 2 Candlesticks of Brass. One of the foresaid Chalesses is sold by William Romynge and Thomas Romynge, with the consent of the parish, for the sum of 111 jl*, and the money thereof was bestowed upon the Church and the Wadeway over the fery 2 years past—WILLIAM RAMSAY, Vicar.

_____

* Four Pounds.

1552. Church Goods, 6th Edward VI. Hayling, South-wood. Inventory of the Goods, Plate, Jewells, Bells, and ornaments of the Church of Hayling, taken the 15th day of July, anno sixto Edwardi, presented by John eye and Thomas Byggs. Item—2 Chaleses of Silver, one gilt with patens, 2 Corpora Clothes, 5 aulter clothes, 6 vestments, 2 Coopes, 2 Candlesticks of Latten, 2 Banner clothes, 2 Stremers. A paull cloth, 4 Towells of Linnen clothe, 4 Bells in the Styple and a little Bell. A payr of Sencors of Latyn, 2 Macers in the Church House remaining for sale.— JOHN WESBY. WILLIAM RAMSAY, Vicar.

1574. Referring to a survey made in 1574, in respect to the coast defences, by the Right Honourable the Earl of Southampton and the Captains for that purpose, they reported: "We find that all the south side of the Isle of Hayling contains, by estimate in length, two long miles. To be upon such flatte as there is no danger of landing, saving at the East and West end thereof. Here two havens, the one called the West Haven, leading to Langston, and the other called the East Haven, leading to the Dell, nere Chichester, in which small Barkes of 60 tons may at the full sea entre if the Maryners be expert, or otherwise very dangerous. At the time Hayling furnished 47 Hable men, 1 corslet,* 7 Harquebusses,† 12 Bows furnished, 17 Bills unfurnished."

From the Manor Rolls in—

1582. Certain offenders were fined four shillings for exercising unlawful games on Sundays and on feast-days, one half going to the lord and the other half to the poor.

1587. Elizabeth—Domestic Papers. Vol. 205, No. 40. Hampshire defences against the Spanish Armada. Certificate of all men furnished and unfurnished within the Hundred of Bosmere. Hayling, Alverstoke and Gosport, under the leading of Thos. Henslow.

1588. 30th May, 1588. Certificate upon survey taken of the County of Southampton, by Captain McDawtrey, touching all the forces, as well as trained and untrained, with

---

* "Corslet." a light armour to protect the breast.
† "Harquebusses," a kind of hand gun.

a brief declaration of the state of the shire : "Many of the men being very rawly furnished, some men lacketh of a headpiece, some a sord, some one thing and some another that is evil, unfit or unbecoming about him."

1650. The Earl of Arundel kept a gamekeeper in the Island at the yearly wages of £6 6s. 8d., and about the same time a Dutchman was sent to Hayling to make a decoy, and the Earl's receiver accounted for £6 2s. 8d. for birds sold at the decoy, beyond 440 sent to London and Albery for the use of the lord.

1650. Royalist Composition papers of Southampton in Hayling: "Thomas Bagshall, son of John Bagshall, seized of one tenement with certain lands, there made his will 18th of March, 1846, of Northstoke, Isle of Hayling, that on the 9th of May, 1650, Thomas Misprat, of Winchester, sequestered the premises for the delinquency of the said John Bagshall. The said Thomas prays to be admitted to the composition, yearly value £10."

1653. The entry of the first marriage in the parish register reads,—"Edward Longford of Northwood, Hailling, husbandman, and Elizabeth Yeoman, of the same, single woman, ware contracted before me Alexander Wilson, Clgm., in the presence of Andrew Powell and——Worm, January 21st."

1664 and 1665. Referring to the Hearth Tax, which was chargeable at Hayling in 16 and 17 Charles II., the following were made :—At North Hayling.

	Hearth charged.		Hearth charged.
Richard Fisher	8	Thomas Seire	3
Thomas Pepson	3	John Reede	1
Andrew Colopes	2	Widow Rogers	1
John Tombes	1	Guy Merth	1
Thomas Roman	4	John Almer	2
William Pay	6	Francis Brown	4
Thomas Perkins	2	Andrew Bucknall, senr.	4
Richard Chevers	4	John Blanchard	3
Richard Perkins	2	M. Andrew Powell (one	
Richard Bilston	3	taken down)	1
Andrew Bucknell, junr.	1	Arthur Vouke	5

	Hearth charged.		Hearth charged.
William Newman	1	Thomas Mew	2
Mrs. Aylinge	1	Widow Burkshall	3
Widow Newman	3	Widow Higgins	3
Stephen Pay	1	Antony Farley	3
John Artherby	2	John Goldinge	3
Thomas Perkins	1	Thomas Bryant	1

SOUTH HAYLING.

Nicholas Perringe	6	Andrew Revell	3
Nicholas Fry	1	Richard Rogers	1
Spinola Dampu	3	Edward Hart	1
Thomas Lone	1	John Carpenter	3
Thomas Perkins	1	William Smith	3
William Long	3	Thomas Jugge	4
Thomas Vengon	2	John Carpenter	2
James Galloway	1		

NOT CHARGEABLE.

John Edwards	2	Clem Millard	1
Widow Vouke	1	John Biggs	1

1679. Parish Register (referring to the antiquity of the Wade-way). "James Biggs drowned in Wad-way, May 15th, 1679, aged 22."

Referring to a Church Brief, we find: "Decr. 1st, 1679, recd. of John Blanchard, Churchwarden of Hayling North, sworn Brief; one for——withe 2s. 6d.; one for——Blandford, for dam wth 1s. 6d.; one for Lurgishall, 1s. 6d.; one for dover, 1s.; one for St. Mary Magdalons, Bormonsey, wth 1s. 6d.; one for Rickmansworth, wth 1s.; one for farlington, 1s. I say recd. by me John Dixon."*

1732. Parish Register, May ye 3rd. Money collected† in this Parish from house to house, for £6,787 and upwards,

---

* It will be seen by this that subscriptions had been made towards seven fires. See Church Brief in future page.
† In response to a Church Brief granted for Stewminster, 1732.

lost by fire at Stewminster, Newton Castle in Con. Dorset. Sum of £0 5s. 4d. by Edward Saunders, Curate.

1750. The Vicarage was valued as a discharged living at a clear yearly sum of £47. The tenths, before the discharge took place, amounted to £17 per annum.

1750. Parish Register, N. H. Burials. Joseph Vicks, from South parish in Hayling; his son Joseph Vicks paid 6s. 8d. for breaking the ground in the church yard of this parish.

1751. None buried. Witness, James Skelton, Vicar.

1758. In the 31st year of George II. a Church Brief was issued, in consequence of a fire at North Hayling, viz.:— "Whereas it has been represented to us as well as by the humble petition of Christopher Smith, Stephen Rogers, and James Croslear, on behalf of themselves and all the Parish of North Hayling Co. of Southampton, and George Bingsley of the City of Chichester, and Robert Woodman of Havant, &c.: that on Wednesday 23rd of March last, there happened a sudden and most dreadful fire which, by the violence of the wind, in the space of three hours the dwelling houses, barns, stables, and other premises with all or the greater part of their household goods were consumed to the value of One thousand one hundred and sixty nine pounds," &c., and asking for alms throughout England and Wales.

Brief to be in force one year.

1759. Fifty-six gallons of brandy were seized as wreck by the tenant of the Duke of Norfolk, and although then and subsequently the Admiralty claimed the right to wreck, it was decided in favour of the lord of the manor. Under a recent Act of Parliament the lord receives compensation from the Admiralty in lieu of wreck.

1762. Parish Register, N. H. Burials. William, son of Thomas Taylor, November 29th, gave notice in writing to ye Officers of the Parish, ty^t ye s^d William Taylor was buried in Woollen.—Off. Curate.

1773. "South'ton. These are to Certify, That at the general Gaol Delivery, held at the Castle of Winchester, in and for the County of Southampton, on Monday, the first day of March instant, before me, whose name is hereunto subscribed, one of His Majesty's Justices assigned to deliver the gaol of the county aforesaid of the prisoners therein, being George Vernell, late of the Parish of Hayling South, in the County Southampton, labourer, tried and convicted of feloniously and burglariously breaking and entering the dwelling house of Elizabeth Crasler, widow (in the night time), situated in the parish aforesaid, and stealing thereout goods and money of the value of seventy pounds and upwards, her property. And that it doth appear to me Joseph Crasler did prosecute the said George Vernell untill he was convicted of the felony and burglary aforesaid, and for a reward unto the said Joseph Crasler upon such conviction, by virtue of an Act of Parliament, made in the tenth and eleventh year of the Reign of His late Majesty King William the Third, intituled 'An Act for the better apprehending prosecuting and punishing of felons that commit burglary housebreaking or robbery in shops warehouses coach-houses or stables or that steal horses,' he the said Joseph Crasler ought to be and is discharged of and from all manner of parish and ward offices within the said parish of Hayling South, wherein the felony and burglary was committed, and this I do hereby certify in order to his being discharged accordingly. Given under my hand this fifth day of March, in the year of Our Lord One thousand seven hundred and seventy-three.

"W. H. ASHHURST."

1777. The grange or farm house, originally in the south-eastern portion of the Island, was rebuilt near the centre of it, probably in consequence of the danger from inundation to which it was exposed in the former situation. There is a tradition that the newer grange was surrounded by a moat enclosing an area of 8 acres. About 30 years ago a cannon ball, a key, a knife studded with fleur-de-lis, and a few coins were said to have been found in cleaning out this moat, but these objects were of doubtful antiquity and authenticity. The grange was finally pulled down in 1777 by Edward Duke of Norfolk. who erected the present Manor House in its place.

1778. A presentment was made that the pound belonging to the manor had been destroyed, and that the lord ought to have it rebuilt. This was done, and it has again recently been restored. The parish stocks were only removed a few years since.

1780. A grant was made to Edward Mitchell of a ware for taking Fishes at Northwood Point for his life, at the yearly rent of 6d.

1790. Memorandum. No burials in the year 1790.

1797. Towards the end of the last century the tenure of the copyhold lands held under the Manor of Hayling, and the payment of tithes, were felt as grievances, and an application was made to the then Duke of Norfolk to take such steps as might be necessary to enable him to enfranchise the copyholds of the manor, and to sell the tithes to which, as lay rector, he was entitled. Accordingly, an Act of Parliament was passed in the year 1797, under which many enfranchisements were effected, the deeds containing a clause by which the tenants of the enfranchised lands were to have the right of taking sea-sand, gravel, and sea-beach from South or Beach Common, for the use and benefit of the enfranchised lands, but for no other purposes. The tithes of the greater part of the Island were purchased by the late Mr. Henry Budd for a large consideration, and he sold them out to small purchasers as opportunities offered.

The ancient rights of free warren and free chase were reserved in the enfranchisements executed by the Duke of Norfolk under the provisions of the Act 37, Geo. III. Of late years, poachers upon Sinah Warren, which is well stocked with rabbits and some few hares, have been convicted before the justices, and the lord still continues to exercise the right.

From 1795 to 1798, the parish register records a great number of burials of persons drowned and unknown.

1798. The Impregnable, man-of-war, ran upon rocks and was lost, the Duke of Norfolk receiving his share as lord; and the timbers of this ship were largely used in the erection of Sinah Farm House, which at that time was the Norfolk Lodge Inn. An Indiaman, probably driven over the bar by stress of weather, went down close to the present western ferry-house.

1805. A vessel from Gibraltar, bound for Penzance, was refused admittance to the harbour in consequence of some infectious disease having broken out among her crew. The master thereupon changed his course for Chichester Harbour; but a heavy storm came on, and the ship was driven on the Poles, nearly in front of Eastock. She was obliged to remain in the position where she had struck, and the coastguard had strict injunctions to shoot the first who came on shore, in order to prevent the spreading of the infection. Provisions were passed from the beach to the vessel by means of a rope. The pestilence increased, and day by day the mortality became greater, until a heavy sea set in from the southward, when the ill-fated vessel foundered, and all on board perished.

1809. Parish Register. Burials. A man unknown; inquest held September 15 by James Greggs. This is the first register of any inquest held under a coroner's inquiry, which was first established in the 3rd Edward I., 1272.

1823. Until the year 1823 the only means of communication with Hayling Island was by means of the east, west, and north ferries, and as these were worked by small boats only, neither cattle nor carriages could enter or leave the place except by ship; and the wade-way passable only at low water, many fatal accidents have happened through being over-powered by the returning tide. The north ferry was free, the ferryman residing from time immemorial in a house on the Island, built at the joint expense of the north and south parishes. In the year last mentioned Mr. William Padwick, of Warblington, a village a little to the north of Hayling, pro-moted an Act of Parliament to form a company for building and making a causeway from Langston, in the Parish of Havant, to the ferry-house in North Hayling, and this Act, which also enabled the company to construct docks, wharves, and quays, was duly passed. The causeway and bridge were opened on the 4th September, 1825, by Bernard Edward Duke of Norfolk, who had contributed to the undertaking.

1825. On February 24th, 1825, an agreement was executed between the same Duke of Norfolk and Mr. Padwick, for the sale of the manor, rectory, and his estates in the Isle of Hayling, and the remainder of the tithes then undisposed of, and, under the terms of this agreement, an Act of Parliament was obtained on the 5th July, 1825, "for vesting the manor, rectory, and Isle of Hayling, in the County of Southampton, part of the settled estates of the Duke of Norfolk, in William Padwick, Esquire, his heirs and assigns, and for applying the money thence arising in the purchase of other estates, to be settled to the same uses, and for other purposes."

By this Act it was recited that the manor, rectory, and estates in the Isle of Hayling, together with tithes remaining unsold. and timber and other trees growing and standing upon the said estates, had been valued at £38,614 5s. 5d., and on payment of this sum into the Bank of England on the 8th May, 1827, the manor, rectory, and estates in the Isle, under the authority of the Act, became vested in and settled upon Mr. Padwick.

According to the schedule to the Act, the property included the Manor of Hayling and the manorial rights ; the rectories of North and South Hayling, with the unsold tithes and the advowson of the vicarage of North and South Hayling; the Manor Farm, with the tide-mill and mill-pond ; Public House Farm, Sinar Common, and Beach Sinar ; the Wholsinar or Shingle Bank ; and a piece of land for a Preventive Service House. The Manor Farm comprised 666 acres, let at a rent of £575 per annum ; the Public House Farm, &c., 190 acres, let at £90 per annum ; and the Wholsinar or Shingle Bank comprised 121 acres, and was stated to be in hand. Out of the estate a modus of £4 8s. was stated to be yearly payable to the Vicar of Hayling in lieu of vicarial tithes.

Direct and easy communication with the main land having been established by means of the bridge, the new lord of the manor inaugurated the first attempt to found a watering-place at Hayling. On the first anniversary of the opening of the bridge (September 4th, 1825) the foundation-stone of a large mansion, which was, and still is, called Norfolk House, was laid, as well as the foundation-stone of another house (or houses) intended as the commencement of a so-called Padwick Terrace. These houses face the beach near the centre of the sea-frontage. The event was celebrated by a public breakfast given by Mr. Padwick to the inhabitants of the Island and many people from Portsmouth. The entertainment, which was given in a large tent on the site of the intended houses, was of a kind very popular fifty years ago. Large quantities of solid food were consumed, and several barrels of beer drank, with somewhat boisterous rejoicing.

About this time Mr. Bromley, a solicitor of London, invested money in building. In a short space of time a convenient hotel, called the Royal Hotel, was erected, together with a building of classical design intended for a library, and also another intended as a bathing establishment; but with the exception of these, and the completion of Norfolk House and the other two houses forming Padwick Terrace, the building scheme was virtually abandoned.

1840. Most unfortunately for the prosperity of the Island, between the years 1840 and 1850 Mr. Padwick entered upon repeated litigation, to an almost unparalleled extent, to establish his real and supposed rights as lord of the manor over the whole Island. Actions were brought with reference to the lordships of the manors of Northstoke, Estoke, and Westhay, and against the copyholders of the manor as to the right to cut and dispose of timber, and the right to free warren, without success. Mr. Padwick also sought to recover lands at Leigh, belonging to Sir George Staunton, under the impression that they had passed to him as part of the Manor of Hayling, and he contended for the right of free warren over a part of Hayling called Bonvilles. The exclusive right of the lord to the fishery, and the right of ferry at the east and west harbours were, in turn, the subject of continued litigation.

1842. The fishermen of Hayling having turned their attention to dredging for oysters, and clearing the soil in order to deposit young oysters for growth and fattening, Mr. Padwick, in 1842, prosecuted certain trespassers and convicted them of stealing and dredging, thus establishing the lord's right to the soil of the oyster beds.

1844. With regard to the fishery, Mr. Padwick brought an action of trespass in 1844, but his claim was negatived by a jury, who, however, confirmed his right to the soil of the creeks. His right to the eastern ferry was not seriously contested; by common law and chancery proceedings he eventually established the right of the lord to the western ferry.

1847. Probably encouraged by the measure of success he had obtained, and apparently actuated by an innate love of litigation, the late Mr. W. Padwick, in the year 1847, made a most extraordinary claim to certain land called " Howard's Furlong," in the Parish of Portsea, covered with houses, and of the estimated value of £200,000. Under the joint opinion of three eminent counsel, he brought 600 actions of ejectment for the recovery of this property as part of the Manor of Hayling. This he was under the necessity of doing at one time in order to save the Statute of Limitations. Two actions that were tried were decided against him, but further litigation thereon ensued, and ultimately the question went to the House of Lords, where the former decisions were confirmed.

1847. In the year 1847 the Portsmouth Branch of the London Brighton and South Coast Railway was opened, and this afforded the inhabitants of Hayling the advantage of railway communication with the South Coast and the Metropolis, by means of the station which was then established at Havant.*

The next attempt to improve the communication between the island and the mainland was by an Act of Parliament for laying a tramway from Hayling Bridge along the causeway northwards to Langston, and thence to the Railway Station at Havant; but from want of funds the powers of this Act were allowed to expire before anything was done to carry it into effect.

1860. The history of the line of railway now successfully in operation from Havant to South Hayling is as singular as anything else connected with a place so remarkable for its vicissitudes as Hayling. This short line of about five miles in length was first promoted by a company formed in 1860,

---

* It was not until 1859 that the South Western Railway was extended to Havant, with running powers over the Brighton line from thence to Portsmouth.

but seven years elapsed before this small but important element in the future prosperity of the Island was completed.

The prime mover in the Hayling Railway Company of 1860, was a Mr. Robert Hume, and the Act authorized the raising of a capital of £50,000 in £10 shares, with £16,000 on mortgage, for constructing a line from a junction with the Brighton and South Western lines at Havant to a point near the west ferry. The line was to be constructed on an embankment in such a manner as to reclaim the mud-lands on the western shore of Hayling, which extend over a space of about 1,100 acres. The bridge or viaduct across the channel from Langston to Hayling Island was to be of open pile-work to the extent of 320 yards, with a swivel opening bridge, having two openings of not less than 40 feet span. The Act allowed three years for purchasing the land, and four years for completing the works; it regulated the tolls and gave power to agree with the South-Western Railway Company for working the line.

1863. The works were soon commenced, Mr. Abernethey being the engineer, and Mr. Furness the contractor; but by the autumn of 1863 it was found necessary to apply to raise additional capital and to extend the time for executing the works, and it was further proposed to extend the railway along the beach to the centre of the Island, and to form docks and a pier at Sinah Ferry, the point fixed upon for the original terminus. On the 14th July, 1864, a further Act, called "The Hayling Railway and Docks Act, 1864," was passed, which sanctioned the raising of £10,000 additional, in £10 shares, for the authorized line; £6,000 in £10 shares for the extension line; £60,000 in £10 shares for the docks and pier; and one-third of each of those amounts beyond on mortgage; and the time for the execution of the railways was extended to two years from the passing of the Act, and for the completion of the docks and pier to five years from that date.

In the month of January, 1865, the portion of the railway from Havant to Langston Harbour was opened for public use, and a considerable traffic in coal, timber, gravel, &c., was carried on. The line of railway being so laid out as to reclaim the mud-land, it became necessary that the embankment through Langston Harbour should be formed on land which is covered with water at every tide, and the difficulty of accomplishing this frustrated the completion of the works, which were more than once swept away by the sea.

Digressing for a while from the progress of the railway, it is necessary to state that Mr. Padwick died on the 10th of September, 1861, leaving a son and three daughters, one of whom, Miss Selina, was a trustee under his will in conjunction with Mr. Gray, a solicitor. The Hayling property had before this time been heavily mortgaged; family differences arose; and Chancery proceedings, on the part of the mortgagees and others, were instituted and carried on for several years. In the course of these proceedings it was found necessary, if possible, to sell the greater part, if not the whole, of the estate, in order to divide the proceeds amongst the parties interested. Arrangements were in fact made in 1864 for selling by auction the Manor and manorial rights, and also the Manor Farm, comprising about 650 acres of land. This sale did not take place; but in August, 1865, the Royal Hotel, 76 acres of freehold, 1,100 acres of mud-land and other property, were put up to auction, but nearly the whole of it was bought in.

1865. Early in the year 1865 the condition of affairs at Hayling attracted the attention of Mr. Francis Fuller, a land surveyor and estate agent, who was well known to the public, not only by the interest he took in matters of social science and philanthropy, but as one of the first and chief of the honoured few who were associated with the late Prince Consort in promoting and organizing the Great Exhibition of all Nations in 1851. The triumphant success of that vast undertaking was greatly aided by Mr. Fuller's zeal, foresight, and confidence, at a time when those qualities were less conspicuous in the majority of its promoters. It would be irrelevant to dwell here upon Mr. Fuller's exertions in promoting the establishment of the Crystal Palace at Sydenham and the Alexandra Palace at Muswell Hill, and other public objects; but his influence on the progress of Hayling Island demands our special notice.

1866. In pursuance of the provision of the Act of Parliament made and passed in the sixth and seventh year of William IV., "An Act for facilitating the Inclosure of Open and Arable Fields in England and Wales," the common fields known as West Hirts, otherwise Westcrofts, Home Field, Stoke Field, and East Stoke Common Fields, were enclosed when the present fields were set out.

1867. Visiting the Island professionally, with reference to the property known to be for sale, Mr. Fuller was struck with its beauty and its capabilities, to the development of which he devoted almost the entire labour of upwards of three years, and a very large expenditure of money. One of the first things which Mr. Fuller applied himself to, whilst negotiating for an extensive purchase of land in the Island, was the completion of the Hayling Railway, as a primary and paramount necessity. With the works suspended and exposed to the action of the sea in every high wind, with an exhausted exchequer and divided councils, the Railway Company was paralysed. It was only by very skilful and delicate negotiation that Mr. Fuller was enabled to infuse new life into the undertaking. He quickly perceived that a line on terra firma, skirting instead of crossing the harbour, would be much more easily and economically made than that which had been authorized, and that it would be desirable to place the terminus near the south beach, rather than at the west end of the Island. · Having become a director of the company, Mr. Fuller caused a Bill to be introduced into Parliament, in the Session of 1867, to authorize the necessary diversion of the line. This Bill passed the House of Lords, but even before it had reached that stage Mr. Fuller proceeded to purchase all the land required, instructed Sir C. Fox & Son to prepare plans for the line, contracted with Mr. F. Furness for its immediate construction, and having seen the works completed, the line supplied with an electric telegraph, and the whole railway approved by the Government Inspector for the Board of Trade, he had the gratification of passing over it from Havant to South Hayling in an experimental train on the 28th of June, 1867, the Bill not having passed the House of Commons, and being in fact rendered unnecessary, from the fact that the line, as finally amended, did not cross any public road, and therefore did not require the sanction of the Legislature.

The Hayling Railway was opened to the public on the 8th July following, and although the traffic was suspended for a few months in the ensuing winter, it was resumed in the spring of 1868 by the contractor, and having since been leased by the London and Brighton Railway Company, it has been worked continuously up to the present time, when there are six trains daily each way between Havant and Hayling.

Mr. Fuller continued to exert himself in various ways to make the resources of the Island known to the public, and made strenuous endeavours to induce capitalists, land and building societies and others, to invest in purchasing and building on the Island.

On the 25th March, 1867, he caused a steeplechase meeting to be held at Eastoke Farm, near the eastern extremity of the Island. This attracted a large number of visitors to the place, and induced Mr. Fuller to follow it up by flat races on the beach, in front of the Royal Hotel, on the 16th and 17th of the following year.

The stewards of the race meeting were Earl Poulett, Viscount St. Vincent, W. G. Craven, Esq., and W. Scott Stonehewer, Esq.; C. J. Longcroft, Esq., of Havant, was treasurer; W. J. F. Verrall, handicapper; and Mr. Marcus Verrall, of Lewes, clerk of the course. A good subscription was made, the Town of Portsmouth, the Stewards, and the late G. G. Sandeman, Esq., of Westfield, South Hayling, contributing £100, as did also Mr. Fuller. There were seven races each day, and the sports, as well as the general arrangements, were excellent.

Additional interest attended the Hayling Races of 1867, from the fact that on the second day the Sultan of Turkey, then on a visit to Her Majesty the Queen, inspected the Fleet at Spithead. Arrangements had been made for a Grand Naval Review, in the course of which the whole fleet steamed out to the Nab Light and back.

1867. Mr. Fuller, moreover, purchased the lease of the Royal Hotel, and had it thoroughly repaired and papered by

Mr. H. R. Trigg, and newly furnished throughout by Messrs. Trollope & Son, of London.

In 1867 he issued an advertisement announcing that three premiums of £100, £50, and £25 respectively would be given for laying out and utilising 200 acres of land on the Island, partly for building, and the remainder as a Park for purposes of recreation; the Park to contain two cricket grounds, with appropriate buildings for players and visitors, to cost not more than £600, and also an archery ground sufficiently spacious for archery meetings on a large scale, with buildings for members and visitors, to cost not more than £400. The competitors were required to devote special attention to the nature, description, and situations of the houses to be erected, either surrounding or in the Park, and to furnish an estimate of the probable ground rent to be realized for the Building Land.

In response to this invitation, 35 sets of designs, embracing in all 87 plans, views, and elevations, were sent. These were arranged for exhibition by Mr. H. R. Trigg, surveyor, of South Hayling, in the building intended for a library,* on the beach, where they excited considerable interest. The number of houses proposed to be erected on the estate varied in the different designs from 28 to 614, the number of acres to be devoted to building from 91 to 193, and the estimated annual ground rent to be realized from £900 to £14,300.

This effort to promote building operations at Hayling was not destined to bear immediate fruit, but there can be no doubt it had an indirect effect in calling public attention to the capabilities of the place.

Throughout the period of Mr. Fuller's connection with the Island he spared neither time nor pains. His proposals to purchase land were for a time favourably received by the officers of the Court of Chancery, and there appeared for a time every prospect of his being able to raise, by the formation of a Joint Stock Company, the large amount necessary to carry out his views, but most unfortunately for him and for the Island, the financial depression which followed the great

---

* Purchased by Mr. Divett and turned into a private residence.

commercial panic of 1866 frustrated all his aims, and after forfeiting a large deposit which he made on account of purchase-money, Mr. Fuller was obliged to abandon his zealous and public-spirited exertions. Mr. Fuller was instrumental in the erection of the West Town Hotel, near the Railway Station.

At this time " Trigg's Monthly Hayling Guide," as well as the fine chromo-lithograph of the future of South Hayling, was issued by H. R. Trigg, surveyor, South Hayling.

1868. In order to settle the affairs of the deceased lord of the manor, it became necessary again to put the property up to public sale, and this was done on the 10th November, 1868, and again on the 6th July, 1869, but on neither occasion with a satisfactory result. The estate was then re-valued by Messrs. D. Smith, Son & Oakley, and once more submitted to auction on the 21st July, 1870. On this occasion a spirited competition took place. The Manor and manorial rights were sold to Osmond Barnard, Esq., of Hay House, Earl's Cove, Essex, who has since sold them to J. C. Parks, Esq., of Upper Teddington, Middlesex. The Manor Farm became the property of William Padwick, Esq., of Thorney Island, which, as shown by the Map, is situated in Chichester Harbour, immediately to the eastward of Hayling.* This gentleman, who, although bearing the same name, is not of the same family as the previous lord, has put the farm into thorough repair and agricultural condition, though it is to be regretted that in doing so he has cut down a large number of ornamental trees. He has also erected several new buildings.

There are three ancient manors—viz., the Hayling Manor, the Havant Manor, and the Manor of Northstoke, Eastoke, and Westhay, with their several lords and rights and privileges. The larger of these is the Hayling Manor, generally alluded to in this work. During Mr. Padwick's life he sought to establish certain rights over the other manors. The recent sale through the Court of Chancery has, it is to be hoped, closed these disputes, for certain sums were allowed to Mr. Barnard in consequence of his not being able to establish the statements put forth. Amongst these was a sum

---

* The remaining lots were shortly afterwards completed by private sale.

of £40 for non-production of a title to the shooting over Eastoke Manor and the right of wreckage over the shore. Mr. Park, the lord of the Manor of Hayling, still claims this wreckage.

The next in extent is the Havant Manor, which occupies a part of North Hayling, the copyholders under which had the right to cut furze, &c., in the Havant Thicket for use upon their copyhold at North Hayling. The present lord is Sir Frederick Fitzwygram, Bart., of Leigh Park, Havant.

The foregoing rights now cease to exist, being purchased by the lord of the manor a few years since.

The least of these manors—viz., the Manor of Northstoke, Eastoke, and Westhay, formerly of greater extent than at present, is singularly situated—Northstoke and Westhay being in the north parish, whilst Eastoke is situate in the south parish, and comprises Eastoke Farm and Eastoke.Common, formerly known as Southwood. These have been recently purchased by Lynch White, Esq., of Leigham House, Streatham, Surrey, in whose possession is an old map, A.D. 1630 (when it was transferred to the Peckham family), showing similar boundaries to the existing ones, having the "Stone Beach" (viz., Sea Beach) included in the measurement of the freehold estate, on which is also defined the old Manor House, at that time of large dimensions, now reduced into cottage tenements; the ancient stone wall clearly indicates its size. The proprietor has allowed me to make extracts from the ancient Court Rolls in his possession.

1870. When Mr. Barnard purchased the manor in 1870, one of his first proceedings was to call the copyholders together, when the lands of the majority of them were enfranchised, with due festive rejoicings, at a banquet at the Royal Hotel; there are some few others to be dealt with in the same way.

The peculiar customs of English manors afford a curious insight into life in the olden time, and the reader may therefore be glad to have the following particulars of the customs of Hayling Island:—

Upon the death of a copyholder intestate his next heir is admitted, and, if a minor, guardianship is granted to his next

6

friend not likely to inherit, upon condition well and honestly
to educate the minor, allowing him competent victuals and
clothes and other necessaries, and keeping the premises in
decent repair, and producing a true account of the profits
when required.   The widow of an intestate copyholder is
admitted to his tenement to hold so long as she shall live
sole, chaste, and unmarried, and pays one penny to the lord
as a fine.   No tenant can let his lands for a longer term than
a year without the lord's licence and paying a fine.

The former lords of Hayling received a fine on the marriage
of their copyhold tenants, and several instances of the payment
of these fines are recorded in the court rolls.

All wreck of the sea, deodands, and goods of felo-de-se
happening within the manor belong to the lord.   Any copyholder is to pay to the lord on death or alienation, a heriot,
namely, his best beast, or, for want of beast, his best in-door
good, and his heir a fine at the will of the lord.   The eldest
son is to inherit after his father, and in case there be no son,
then the eldest daughter; and in like manner amongst colla-
terals.   For every horse turned loose in the lanes the owner
ought to pay to the lord sixpence; for every hog, threepence;
and for every sheep, twopence.   Every person who shall cause
gravel to be carried from that part of the land called Ferry-
house Point, shall forfeit and pay to the lord two shillings and
sixpence for every cart-load.

The ancient court leet of the manor has fallen into disuse, and the court baron is only convened when occasion
requires it.

The court rolls of the manor, extending backward to a very
early period, are preserved, some in the Tower, some in the
Rolls Chapel, and some in the custody of the Duke of
Norfolk, others having been lost in the transitional periods
of its history.   These contain many curious presentments in
reference to timber, wreck of the sea, treasure trove, free
warren, and the fisheries, as well as with reference to offences
committed within the manor.

Before concluding our historical notes, we may observe that
the peculiar rights of the copyholders have done much to
retard the march of progress.

Amongst others now interested in the development of the resources of the Island are Mr. C. J. Park, the present lord of the manor, Mr. Sandeman, Capt. Staunton, Wm. Padwick, Esq., and D. P. McEwen, Esq.

1873. The first Regatta, and which was hoped to have been the forerunner of an annual series of such agreeable gatherings, was held on the 13th of August, 1873, conducted by a spirited committee—Mr. H. R. Trigg, acting as hon. sec. The gun-boat Earnest was kindly placed at the disposal of the Committee by Admiral Sir Rodney Mundy, K.C.B., and the entries for the different matches were very numerous; not only Portsmouth and Hayling, but Southsea, Gosport, Pilsey, Emsworth, Bosham, Cowes, Ryde, Shoreham, Brighton, and London being represented amongst the competitors. The prizes consisted of silver cups, new boats, and money to the value of £96 5s. This and two subsequent ones, 1874 and 1877, were highly commented upon by the several London and local papers.

1873. The First Administrative Battalion Hants Rifle Volunteers, under their colonel, Sir W. H. Humphrey, first pitched their tents here.

In September, 1873, a meeting of the copyholders was held for the purpose of considering the offer of the lord of the manor to buy up all rights or supposed rights of copyholders over the South Beach. Much opposition was made to the scheme, Mr. Harris making an exorbitant claim for his rights, whilst he valued those of others infinitesimally small. This and other kindred opposition again barred improvements at Hayling.

1873. In November of this year the common land known as Stoke Common Land was enclosed, setting out a road from a point nearly opposite Stoke Wind Mill to North Hayling Railway Station.

In the same year an Act called the "Southsea and Hayling Tramways and Ferry Act" was obtained for the purpose of laying down a tramway from Southsea Pier, passing through Eastney, crossing Langston Harbour by steam ferry, and continuing the tramway past the Royal Hotel, and terminating at Rails Lane, east of the Coastguard Station.

The foregoing Act was abandoned.

1875. In August, 1875, under the Act for enclosure of open fields in England and Wales, Verner Common Field was enclosed, and allotments made to the several owners. Shortly after the several lots were purchased by the late lord of the manor, C. J. Park, Esq., who has since then prosecuted persons for cutting furze and underwood thereon.

1877. In January of this year the water mill was destroyed by fire. Its antiquity is unquestionable, for in the 22nd of Edward I. (1294) it was taken, with the manor, &c., by the Crown from the Abbey of St. Peter's of Jumièges. At this time it was valued at 60s. per annum. In 1541 it was leased to John Tawke, when the sum of £55 14s. was expended for reconstruction and repairs.

About this time the salterns, which are mentioned in Domesday Book as belonging to Ulward, the friar, became so dilapidated that they ceased to be used for that purpose.

For a few weeks a steam launch plied across Langston Harbour in place of the small ferry boats.

Two companies were registered to supply Hayling with gas, one called the Hayling Island Gas Company, the other the South Hayling Gas and Coal Company. Neither of the companies floated. Gasworks were, however, constructed by private enterprise, Mr. H. R. Trigg, being the present proprietor.

1878. South Hayling was declared one of the contributory places under the Guardians of Havant Union, acting as the Rural Sanitary Authority.

1883. In August, an Act came into operation to erect a bridge across Langston Harbour to connect the Island with Southsea. The bridge was to have a swing opening of 40 ft. The plans met with the approval of the Government; the capital was £50,000, much of which was subscribed; but further disputes between the owners of the soil and the copyholders resulted in the withdrawal of the capital and a stay to the development of South Hayling.

1885 and **1886.** Several important meetings of the copyholders and others interested in the improvements of Hayling were held. A scheme was proposed to transfer all existing or presumed right over the South Beach, whether belonging to the owners of the soil or copyholders, into the hands of conservators, for the purpose of regulating and adapting its use to the public. The scheme met with the support of the Land Commissioners, who prepared an Act to go before the House of Commons. This, however, was withdrawn in consequence of the strong opposition given to it by the Rev. J. A. Bell, the Vicar, Lord R. B. Bruce, T. Harris, Esq., and others. This also caused the projected floating bridge and railway scheme of constructing a railway from South Hayling Railway Station to Fratton Station, in the Parish of Portsea, with a swing bridge crossing Langston Harbour, to be abandoned. The bridge was to have been constructed for railway and road traffic. This Act was also obtained, but eventually abandoned through the continued difference.

1888. Further disputes arose respecting asserted rights over "Verner Common," otherwise Verner Common Land, by reputed commoners and others. These resulted in the prosecution and fining of one William Grist for wilful and malicious damage by cutting underwood. Further prosecutions followed, when four others were fined, and W. Grist imprisoned for fourteen days.

1890. Further contention took place between the copyholders and owners of the soil, resulting in the destruction of fencing.

1891. Renewed attempts were made to establish a bridge between Hayling and Southsea. The continued opposition of copyholders had much weight in preventing the necessary capital being subscribed.

CHAPTER III.

A FORTNIGHT AT HAYLING;

or, Suggestions for Daily Excursions in the Neighbourhood.

1st day—Havant, Warblington, Emsworth, Bosham.
2nd day—Leigh Park, Rowland's Castle, Stanstead, Idsworth.
3rd day—West Leigh, Horndean, Catherington, Waterloo, Purbrook Belmont, and Bedhampton.
4th day—Cumberland Fort, Southsea, Landport, Portsmouth.
5th day—Isle of Wight.
6th day—Chichester.
7th day—Arundel.
8th day—Southampton, Bishop's Waltham.
9th day—Winchester and its vicinity.
10th day—Portchester Castle.
11th day—Salisbury.
12th day—Portsmouth, by Road, Bedhampton, Cosham, Wymering, Kingston, Milton.
13th day—Trip by Steamboat round the Isle of Wight.
14th day—Wittering.

SO numerous and important are the objects of interest in the neighbourhood of Hayling, that it may be useful to indicate to visitors a number of Excursions which may each be made in the course of a single day, pointing out the routes to be taken, and the places to be visited on each occasion.

First Day.

Havant, Warblington, Emsworth, Bosham.

By traversing the short line of the Hayling Railway, from South to North Hayling and Langston, we arrive in about fifteen minutes at

HAVANT.—This is a clean and thriving town, with a population, in 1871, of 2,634. The road through it from north to south occupies the line of an old Roman road from Winchester to the coast, and several Roman remains have been found in it. Its name, Have-hunt, is of Saxon derivation, and, like Boar-hunt, in the same county, points to the forestal nature of the country in early times. At the compilation of Domesday Book, Havant belonged to the monks of Winchester. King John granted the monks a market, and Bishop Waynflete obtained a confirmation of this, together with a two days' fair, now held on the 17th October and the 22nd June. The church appears to have occupied the site of a Roman temple or other edifice, some foundations of which, together with Roman coins, were found during some repairs in 1832. In early times there was a palace attached to it, for the occasional residence of the Bishops of Winchester. The church (which has been called a quarter cathedral) is dedicated to St. Faith, a lady of Gaul, who suffered martyrdom about the year 290; and a preceding church so dedicated existed here as early as the year 1100. The crypt under St. Paul's Cathedral, London, which dates from the year 610, was the first church in England known to have been dedicated to St. Faith. The present church is cruciform, consisting of a nave and chancel, with side-aisles and transept, and a square embattled tower, having a massive buttress at each angle to counteract an original settlement, and a turret staircase at the north-east angle. The pillars of the tower are of the Norman era, with rudely sculptured capitals, and support plain Early-English arches. The chancel was rebuilt by William of Wykeham about 1400, the windows being of the Perpendicular style. The churchyard covers an acre of ground, and, from the accumulated burials of centuries, its surface is much above the adjoining streets. The Rev. Prebendary Renaud, M.A., is the present Rector of Havant. The church has been substantially repaired and enlarged. A Town Hall was erected at Havant about 1868, from the designs of Mr. Drew. A new parochial school for boys and girls has also been erected at Brockhampton. About seventeen years ago a cemetery was consecrated and opened to the north of the town. At Red Hill, in the parish of Havant, there is a district church, dedicated to St. John the Baptist, with parsonage-house and school. The workhouse of the Havant Union, of which Hayling forms a part, is situate in West Street in this town. There are several malt-houses and breweries in Havant, and some fell-mongers' yards. The principal inns are the Bear and the Dolphin. In the old posting days the Bear, being on the road from Portsmouth to Chichester and Arundel, had a larger business than at present; it is still an excellent inn. The Queen and other members of the Royal Family frequently changed horses there *en route* from Osborne to Arundel Castle and Goodwood.

A pleasant walk of half a mile along the high road leads from Havant to Warblington, a parish to the east of Havant and the north of Langston. From the twelfth to the fourteenth centuries the manor belonged to the De Warblingtons, who took their name from the place. Henry III. granted a market and fair to Emsworth, a village in the parish. The former is discontinued; but the fair, with others subsequently granted, is still held. Warblington Church is a large and interesting cruciform structure, built in the early part of the fourteenth century, when the Early English architecture merged into the Decorated. It is dedicated to St. Thomas a'Becket, and stands in a spacious churchyard, where there is a yew-tree of very great age, the trunk measuring 26 feet in circumference. The chancel contains a number of ancient stone coffins, and some interesting specimens of ancient glazed tiles, comprising ten different patterns, in the pavement. There is also a hagioscope in perfect preservation. The north porch is constructed of massive timber, coeval with the building. It is of exceedingly beautiful design and proportions, and is ornamented with ogee trefoils and lattice-work. This porch has been engraved in "The Glossary of Architecture." The Rev. — Norris is Rector of Warblington.

Close to the church, and forming a pleasing group with it, are the remains of a castle, which appears to have been erected about the same time as the church, and which in 1552 belonged to Sir Richard Cotton, who entertained Edward VI. here on his journey to the coast. The remains consist only of a brick tower and gateway, faced with stone and festooned with ivy. The castle was originally quadrangular, 200 feet in length and breadth, enclosing a central court. It was probably dismantled in 1642 by Sir William Waller, the Parliamentary leader, when he besieged Portsmouth and took Chichester from the Royalists. Its materials were dispersed over the neighbourhood, and may be traced, not only in the farm-house and buildings at Warblington, but in various old houses in Hayling, Havant and Emsworth, and even in Portsmouth, where there are streets called Warblington and Havant Streets.

The remains of an ancient water mill attached to the castle may still be traced, but a beautiful moat, which until recently surrounded the ruins, has unfortunately been levelled by the owners of the property.

A walk of a mile and a half through pleasant fields leads in an easterly direction to

EMSWORTH, a village at the eastern extremity of the parish, on a stream called the Ems, which divides Hampshire from Sussex. The east passage of Langston Harbour runs up to it, and affords great natural accommodation to the colliers and coasting vessels trading to the port. There is a ship-building yard here, where vessels of considerable size are built: one of upwards of 400 tons was launched here in 1848. There is a church dedicated to St. James. The chapel of ease, dedicated to St. Peter, and built by private subscription, after laying many years in disuse, has been converted by the Emsworth Proprietary Hall Association into a spacious Lecture Hall. Emsworth has also a custom-house and railway-station. The population of Warblington, including Emsworth, was 2,438 in 1871. The harbour of Emsworth has, from an early date, been celebrated for its oysters.

There is a Fishermen's Dredging Society here, which has obtained a grant from the Board of Trade of the exclusive right to its members to lay down and dredge oysters over a portion of Langston Harbour, about a mile and a half in length by the width of the tidal channel. This space is indicated by buoys. The late Mr. Jarman, of Emsworth, had a similar grant to himself of about one mile in length. Emsworth Station is the first from Havant on the line of the Brighton Railway.

BOSHAM is a village three miles further east of Emsworth, and here there is another station. Bosham is a place which should on no account be left unseen by visitors in this neighbourhood. There is known to have been a monastery here in the year 680. Canute had a castle here, and his daughter, it is said with strong probability, was buried in the church of the monastery. It was from this place that Harold sailed on his ill-fated voyage to Normandy. The church has recently been restored, and during the process of restoration some interesting discoveries were made. Several windows, which evidently date from a period anterior to the Norman Conquest, were opened, and some stone and chalk coffins of very remote antiquity were found. One of these is conjectured to have contained the body of Canute's daughter. There is a small crypt under the church, a very fine old font, and the tombs of Herbert de Boscham, who was secretary to Thomas a'Becket. The church so associated with the memory of the unfortunate Harold is represented in the famous tapestry, which is now preserved in the Hotel of the Prefecture of Bayeux, known under the name of "Toile de St. Jean," consisting of a piece of brownish linen cloth, two hundred and fourteen feet long and twenty inches wide, worked with woollen threads of different colours, as bright and distinct, and the letters of the superscription as legible, as if the work of yesterday. It is held that the tower of the church is of that construction to leave little doubt of its being the same that existed when the church was entered by Harold.

After the day's excursion thus planned, it will be advisable to make the return journey by train from Bosham to South Hayling.*

Second Day.

Leigh Park, Stanstead, Rowland's Castle, Idsworth.

LEIGH PARK, which is within one and a half miles from Havant, is one of the most magnificent seats in the South

---

* Bosham may be reached from Hayling, by pleasure boat, at all times of the tide.

of England. As a careful inspection of the beautiful grounds, conservatories, and hot houses, will require several hours, and will richly reward the time bestowed upon it, it will be necessary to drive by road from Hayling, via Havant, to Leigh Park, and also from thence to the other places included in the programme for the day; train could be taken to Havant, and vehicle from thence.

Leigh Park was formerly the property of Sir George Staunton, Bart., from whose representatives it was purchased about eight years ago by Wm. Henry Stone, Esq., then M.P. for Portsmouth, who has added largely to the estate, and, after pulling down the former mansion, erected an entirely new one on a more commanding site, from the designs of Mr. R. W. Drew, Architect, of London. This house is of red brick with stone dressings, and commands extensive views in every direction. The principal apartments are spacious, and the general design in the highest degree effective. With the conservatory, lodges, and stables, the entire cost of the buildings exceeded £20,000, which property Mr. Stone sold to Major-General Sir F. Fitzwygram, Bart., M.P. for South Hants.

The estate comprises in all about 2,500 acres, including Havernacke Thicket, which extends to 900 acres, and the garden and pleasure grounds, which occupy not less than 25 acres. With a rare degree of liberality, Major-General Sir F. Fitzwygram, Bart., throws his grounds open to the public on holidays and other special occasions; and that the privilege is highly valued by the residents of Portsmouth and the neighbourhood is shown by the fact that on Coronation Day (June 28th, 1867) the number present was upwards of 20,000. Of course the great majority of these belong to the working-classes, and here as elsewhere the same testimony is borne to the good and orderly conduct of these gatherings of the people. Not a flower is plucked nor a tree or shrub injured. The attendance of the police either in or out of uniform is unnecessary, and the more numerous the visitors the less appears to be even the risk of injury to the place. Two days' work, with a few extra gardeners, suffices to remove all traces of an assemblage so vast as that last mentioned.

The following are some of the particular attractions of this splendid park and grounds, but a personal visit can alone realize more than a faint conception of their rare, and in many cases unique, beauty :—

In the open grounds are some remarkable fine cedars, pines, and other ornamental trees, among which may be enumerated a very fine *Picea Pinsapo*, grand specimens of *Cedrus Deodara*, *Abies Douglassii*, *Abies Morinda*, *Araucaria Imbricata* and *Excelsa*, *Cryptomeria Japonica*, *Picea Nobilis*, *Picea Nordmanniana*, *Silisburia Adiantifolia*, or *Maiden-hair Tree*, *Mangolia Thomsonæ* and *Grandiflora*, *Callalpa Syrinæfolia*, *Alianthus Glandulosa*, *Arbutus Procera* and *Liriodendron Tulipifera*. Besides an extremely beautiful and interesting collection of gold and silver ferns, raised from seed ripened at Leigh Park, there are beautiful specimens of the following, amongst numerous other exotic ferns— *Dicksonia Antarctica*, *Alsophylla Australis*, *Cyathea Dealbata Excelsa*, *Australis* and *Smithii*, &c. The heaths and azaleas are of the choicest description, and in one large old conservatory is a wonderful collection of camellias, oranges, lemons, citrons, &c., one orange tree in the present summer being loaded to profusion with its rich and golden fruit. The collection of orchids is very fine and extensive, and includes the first plant of *Cartupodium Punctatum* which flowered in the British Islands. Omitting all notice of the pineries, graperies and peach-houses, which are each and all as perfect as nature and art can make them, we may allude to the very fine collection of aquatic plants. These, which occupy several spacious tanks, are in luxurious perfection. They include the *Papyrus Aquifolium*, or Bulrush of the Nile, which flowers freely ; and also the true *Nelumbium Speciosum*, or sacred bean of the Egyptians. There is also a very fine double variety of this which far surpasses the other, the flower being larger, quite double, and of a brighter colour. The seed of both varieties has been ripened here. There is also a fine specimen of *Orya Sativa*, the rice of commerce (which, from the luxuriant growth it is making, seems to delight in the warmth and moisture), and several good plants of *Ouvirandra Fenestralis*, the lace or lattice plant, the leaves of which are subdivided by a fine net-work of veins resembing a piece of lace. The water lilies are remarkably fine, *Nymphea Dentata*, *Ceralea*, *Devoniensis*, &c., flourishing and showing flowers and foliage of immense size and dazzling beauty. We must close our notice with a reference to the *Victoria Regia*. This queen of aquatic plants was, with equal taste and propriety, dedicated to and named after the Queen by its discoverer, Sir Robert Schomburg, who found it growing in a currentless basin in the River Berbice, in British Guiana, South America, in 1837. It was first flowered by Sir Joseph Paxton at Chatsworth, and there were formerly two specimens, which also flowered at the Crystal Palace. Only one flower opens at a time, lasting only two days in beauty. When it first opens it is pure white with a pink centre. In from six to ten hours the pink colour gradually extends over the whole flower, so that in eighteen hours it is changed to a pinky rose colour. A single flower, when full blown, measures 18 inches in diameter, and diffuses a strong and sweet perfume.

The calyx has four leaves, the corolla from 80 to 100 petals. Not less beautiful or wonderful are the leaves. These are produced on stalks of from 10 to 12 feet in length and 3 inches in circumference The leaves are circular, light green above and vivid crimson below, closely studded with prickles three-quarters of an inch long; and on the 1st August, 1863, the specimen at Leigh Park, which is the finest in the kingdom and flowers freely, had eleven leaves floating on the surface of the tank, four of which measured each 7 feet 4 inches in diameter, exclusive of the beautiful raised rim, which was 2 inches wide, making the total circumference of each leaf 22 feet 6 inches.

From Leigh Park the journey by Red Hill to Stanstead Park is one and a quarter miles. Stanstead House is a very beautiful seat, and owes much of its attraction to the taste and liberality of the late Charles Dixon, Esq., who died in 1852. For some time afterwards that gentleman's widow remained at Stanstead, but the house is now in the occupation of G. Wilder, Esq. The property includes about 1,000 acres, in the Parish of Stoughton.

Attached to Stanstead Estate is Stanstead College, a structure in the Elizabethan style, founded in 1850 by Mr. Dixon for the reception of six decayed wine merchants of the cities of London, Liverpool, or Bristol, each of whom receives £50 a year, beside a residence, medical attendance, &c.; £50 a year being also secured for another decayed merchant and his wife, as superintendents. The ground comprises five acres; the building cost over £6,000, is surrounded by a terrace walk, and contains a vestibule for indoor exercise, and a common dining hall; it is endowed with £20,000 invested in the public funds. Mrs. Dixon, in pursuance of her husband's wish, erected a school for boys and girls, and a fund has been bequeathed by Mr. Dixon which enables these children to pay an annual visit for a few days to the sea coast, for the advantages of bathing, and otherwise maintaining or recruiting their health. On several occasions Hayling has been selected as the locality for carrying out this benevolent purpose. Close at hand are some remains, known as

ROWLAND'S CASTLE, consisting of two large masses of wall, 10 feet in thickness, composed of flint, undressed stone, chalk and mortar, and a postern entrance, with distinct traces of a moat and fosse. Roman coins and pottery, and the remains of a Roman villa, have been found at Rowland's

Castle, proving that it must have been a Roman station of some importance. Here was probably a castle in the Saxon period,which was occupied until Warblington Castle was erected. There is a tradition that there was formerly a subterranean communication between Rowland's Castle and the Castle at Warblington. Another brief trip conducts us northwards to

IDSWORTH, the seat of Sir J. Clark Jervoise, Bart. This occupies a most romantic and picturesque site in a deep valley, amidst avenues of beech trees, and is also surrounded by beautiful grounds, the park being well stocked with deer and game.

In the park there is an ancient chapel, partly in the early English style ; here are two frescoes in the chancel, one an event in the life of St. Herbert, the other the presentation of the head of St. John the Baptist. Idsworth House is a handsome structure in the Elizabethan style.

It must be stated that previous application should be made to the respective proprietors of Stanstead and Idsworth for permission to visit those places.

The return journey from Idsworth to Hayling, by road, covers a distance of nine miles. Train can be taken from Rowland's Castle to Havant, thence to Hayling.

Third Day.

West Leigh, Horndean, Catherington, Waterloo, Purbrook,
Belmont, Bedhampton.

To complete our survey of the interesting localities in the near neighbourhood of Hayling, before proceeding to more distant attractions, a third Excursion may well be made to the places above named, and in order to do so it will be necessary to drive by road.

WEST LEIGH HOUSE, is a small but very agreeable place, occupied by H. F. Earle, Esq. This, as well as the other seats named in this day's Excursion, can be seen by permission of the owners. From thence a journey of three miles brings us to

CATHERINGTON, a very pretty village of 1,293 inhabitants. The most populous part of the parish is called Horndean; the celebrated Horndean Ale Brewery is in the centre of the village.

The Church of St. Catherine is an ancient structure, with a square tower containing five bells. Here are the monuments of the celebrated tragedian, Edmond Kean, and his wife, and of his son, Charles Kean; Sir Nicholas Hyde, Chief Justice of England; Lord Clarendon, and Admiral Sir Charles Napier. Catherington House was built by the first Viscount Hood. Queen Caroline was entertained here, previous to her trial. The marriage of the Duke of York, afterwards James II., with Ann Hyde, took place here.

Making our return on the Old Portsmouth Road, through the Forest of Bere, we arrive at Waterloo. The church is a small structure of early English style; here is a memorial window inserted in the west side to the late Sir Charles Napier. The Industrial School at Stakes was built by J. Deverell, Esq., of Purbrook Park, the lord of the manor. Farlington House is a handsome modern dwelling with tasteful grounds. Farlington Church, originally built in the 12th century, has a memorial chancel, the ground roof and marble pillars are strikingly beautiful, the painted window being an object of admiration and worthy of inspection. On our return we must slightly divert from the road to mount the celebrated Portsdown Hill, near Belmont. We shall here be repaid well for our trouble in beholding one of the most charming views in the South of England (surpassing the celebrated view from Richmond hill, and at Devizes). After having feasted our eyes upon the magnificent Panorama of Sea View, we will, by the courtesy of Mr. Snooke, enter by the lodge gate, and there behold an inland view of almost surpassing grandeur. Reluctantly we leave this view of views and proceed homeward via Havant.

Fourth Day.

Cumberland Fort, Southsea, Portsea and Portsmouth.

Respecting the Island of Portsea (see Map), comprising Portsmouth, Portsea, Landport, and Southsea, many volumes have been written, and many more would be required to describe all the peculiarites of so remarkable a district, with the alterations which take place in it from year to year.

Its vicinity to Hayling renders it far too important to be overlooked by the visitor desiring to make himself acquainted with the surroundings of that place.

PORTSEA ISLAND may be reached either by railway from Hayling, via Havant, or by the western ferry and Southsea. Assuming the latter route to be taken, on landing from the Ferry, we first reach Cumberland Fort, a strong work erected for the defence of the Channel, commenced in 1746, but not brought into an efficient state till 1820. This fortress mounts 120 heavy guns, and is capable of accommodating 3,000 men in garrison. It is occupied by the Royal Marine Artillery, whose shell practice across the channel at a target three or four miles distant is seen to great effect ; we need hardly add, it is heard on Hayling Beach.

From Fort Cumberland to Southsea the distance is about two and a half miles, and the only mode of conveyance between these points is by a fly or other specially hired vehicle. The two places have recently been connected by means of a splendid esplanade, which effectually prevents encroachments of the sea, and also forms a continuation of the esplanade along the beach between the fortifications of Portsmouth and Southsea Castle. The favourable consideration of this proposal by the Board of Admiralty and the War Department was promised in 1867. On arriving at

SOUTHSEA, the Castle, the Beach, the fine open Common the Pier, and other features of the locality, compel the attention of the visitor ; but it is not the province of a work like the present to dwell upon them in detail.

The pier and beach at Southsea command a view of the unrivalled roadstead at Spithead, where, it has been estimated, a thousand ships of the line might anchor without inconvenience.

From this pier the journey to Landport may be made either by road or by the tramway in connection with the joint station of the Brighton and South Western Railways.

The harbour, the fortifications, and the public buildings of Portsmouth are objects of the deepest interest, and in addition to these the military works on Portsdown Hill, and the huge detached sea forts at distances varying from half a mile to six miles from the shore, will attract due notice from their magnitude and importance. Portsmouth Dockyard, the greatest Naval Arsenal of England, is shown on personal application at the gates, any day between 9 a.m. and 5 p.m., visitors signing their names in a book kept for that purpose. Visitors are conducted, free of charge, over the whole of the establishment.* The Royal Clarence Victualling Yard, containing the ingenious machinery used in the manufacture of biscuits for the Navy, may be inspected with equal facility. The Gun Wharf, with its series of storehouses for munitions of war, and the Haslar Gunboat Slip-way offer peculiar attractions; whilst the famous Victory in the harbour, the historical flag-ship of the immortal Nelson, cannot fail to be seen with the greatest interest and emotion by any one who is not insensible to the glory of the British Navy.

Near the Railway Station is the Public Park of Portsmouth, for which the town is mainly indebted to the intervention of Mr. Francis Fuller. The extent of this park is but a few acres. For many years, up to and including 1866, this space, which belonged to the War Department, had been suffered to go out of use, and to become neglected, in spite of many attempts to obtain its appropriation to purposes calculated to benefit the town. In the year last mentioned Mr. Fuller's attention was drawn to this neglected site, and with the greatest promptitude, and not a little tact and good feeling, he addressed the late General Grey, the Private Secretary to Her Majesty the Queen, pointing out the

---

* See Lewis's shilling "Hand Book of Portsmouth and Guide to Dockyard and other Government Establishments."

7

importance of a public park to the crowded denizens of Portsmouth, and the ease with which the land in question could be applied to such a purpose. Her Majesty at once instructed General Grey to bring Mr. Fuller's communication before the authorities of the War and Ordnance Department; and in a few weeks, Mr. E. Emanuel, who was then Mayor of Portsmouth, had the gratification of receiving an official intimation that this happy suggestion would be carried out. The readiness with which Her Majesty attended to a proposition so important to the moral and physical welfare of her subjects in this locality—allowing it further to be named "The Victoria Park"—is only one of numerous acts which have entitled her to the devoted and affectionate loyalty of her people.

Assuming the journey to Portsmouth to have commenced at the West Ferry, Hayling, the return may be made by railway in little more than half an hour.

Fifth Day.

THE ISLE OF WIGHT—To visit which we must take the first train from Hayling to Portsmouth and meet the first boat from Southsea Pier.

The charming aspect of the Isle of Wight, as seen from Hayling Beach, is a daily invitation to those who are strangers to it to realize its beauties by a nearer view, and at the same time a constant reminder to those already familiar with them; whilst even after dusk the twinkling Nab Light and the Warner proclaim the existence of the lovely Isle.

The accessibility from Hayling of Ryde and Cowes, and, through those towns, of all the principal places in the Isle of Wight, renders the voyage, in fine weather, an almost irresistible temptation.

In the summer season the steamboats run from Southsea Pier eight times a day, the voyage to Ryde occupying about 25 minutes, and from thence to Cowes about 20 minutes more; whilst the times at which they return to Southsea are so arranged, that with the aid of the railways in the Island, a great portion of the interior, or as may be preferred, the western, eastern, or southern coast, may be visited from Hayling in a single day's excursion.

Sixth Day.

CHICHESTER.—To have a long day we must take an early train from Hayling.

To the lover of our ancient architecture, Hayling possesses the great advantage of being within easy distance of three Cathedrals, those of Chichester, Winchester, and Salisbury— these being among the most interesting and important of any in the kingdom.

Chichester is only nine miles to the east from Havant, on the line of the London and Brighton Railway, and it is also accessible by water from Chichester Harbour, on the east side of the Island. It occupies the site of the Roman station called Regnum, and its existing walls, which are of great extent, are constructed chiefly of Roman materials. The Cathedral, built in the thirteenth century, retains some specimens of Norman architecture, but it is chiefly early English. Its total length is 427 feet, that of the transept 129 feet, and the church is remarkable for having double aisles. The spire, which was erected in the fourteenth century, rose to a height of 300 feet. This, with a portion of the tower, fell to the ground whilst some repairs were being made to the Cathedral, on the 21st of February, 1861; but the whole was rebuilt in the most durable and substantial manner, under the superintendence of Sir George Gilbert Scott, R.A., in the short space of five years and a half, the cap-stone having been placed on the summit of the, new spire by the Bishop of the Diocese on the 28th June, 1866. The reputation of the distinguished architect employed is a guarantee that the work has been carried out in strict conformity with the original design; and it is honourable to the public spirit of the ecclesiastical and municipal authorities of Chichester, aided by the Duke of Richmond and the nobility and gentry, as well as the public generally of the district, that

the large sum necessary for the work was so promptly raised.
The original contract for the restoration amounted to about
£58,000, but this was subsequently increased by the restoration
of the roofing and vaulting of the nave, choir, and transepts,
and other works in the Cathedral.   There are monuments of
Bishop Ralfe, Saffred, St. Richard, 1253, Arundel, 1478,
Sherburne and Storey, 1592, Hurdis and others of later date.
In the south transept are some curious historical paintings of
the time of Henry III.   There is also a monument to the
memory of Collins, the poet, who was a native of Chichester.
Near the Cathedral is a bell tower with massive walls 120 feet
high, called Ryman's Tower.   Chichester Market Cross, erected
at the close of the fifteenth century by Bishop Storey, is one of
the finest and most elaborately ornamented market crosses
remaining in England.   It is of large size and pleasing
proportions.   The city had a population in 1851 of 8,662.

The present Bishop of Chichester is the Rt. Rev. Dr.
Durnford, and the Very Rev. J. W. Burgon is Dean.   Within
about four miles from Chichester is

GOODWOOD—the renowned seat of the Duke of Richmond,
annually the scene of the famous races, established in 1803,
which are unequalled in the world for the natural attractions
and fashionable accessories with which they are graced.

Seventh Day.

Arundel Castle.

Easily accessible from Hayling by the London and Brighton
Railway are the town and castle of Arundel, the Arundel
Station being 24 miles from South Hayling.

ARUNDEL CASTLE is most imposing from its magnitude,
magnificence, and picturesque site, and highly interesting from
its feudal associations.   It is the chief seat of the Duke of
Norfolk and Earl of Arundel, and stands on the verge of a
plateau which sinks precipitously on two sides at least 20 feet
to the bank of the river Arun ; on the right bank of which,

and on the slope of the hill leading to the castle, stands the town of Arundel. The position of the castle is a strong one, and was formerly well fitted to command the surrounding country. It is supposed there was a castle here in Saxon times, and the next is known to have been built by Roger de Mortimer, soon after the Norman Conquest. It has been the scene of various historical events; and in the civil wars of Charles I. was taken by the Parliamentary army, retaken by the Royalists, and again captured by the Protector's forces. A considerable portion of the old castle still exists, but the principal part of the present edifice was built, towards the close of the last century, by Charles, eleventh Duke of Norfolk. Subsequently it was neglected by its noble owners; but from 1842 to 1864 the work of restoration was continuously carried on, at a total cost of not less than £100,000; and Arundel Castle, with its park and grounds, is now one of the most perfect places of the kind in England. The buildings cover an area of five acres, and many of them derive a peculiar charm from the rich mantle of ivy and ornamental foliage with which they are clothed. Some of the state apartments are remarkable for their dimensions. The Long Gallery is 195 feet long by 12 feet wide. In the Baron's Hall, 115 feet by 35, is a fine painted window of the signing of Magna Charta, by Backler. The keep and part of the walls are the only relics of the ancient edifice. The park comprises 1,245 acres, and contains many hundred of deer; it is much frequented by visitors, and, with the ancient keep and new dairy, is open to the public on Monday and Friday only. The Fitzallan Chapel contains the tombs of the illustrious Princes of the houses of Fitzallan and Howard; here is also the tomb of Eleanor, Countess of Arundel, 1418. Many of the Dukes and Duchesses of Norfolk and the Earls of Arundel are buried in the vaults beneath the Lodge Chapel. Arundel Park is visited by many thousands of people on bank and other holidays, availing themselves of the excursion trains run by the Brighton Railway Company from Portsmouth, Havant, Brighton, and the intervening and adjacent towns. The population of Arundel in 1851 was 2,748.

A large Roman Catholic Cathedral has now been erected

in the grounds of the castle, from the designs of Sir G. G. Scott, R.A. The cost of its erection has been upwards of £50,000, and the works have been executed by Mr. George Myers, of London.

Eighth Day.

SOUTHAMPTON can be reached either by the South Western Rail from Havant, or by (the far more agreeable route) steamboat from Portsmouth or Southsea Pier. It would be advisable to take early train from Hayling. Taking the steamboat we pass Spithead, and steam up the Solent and beautiful Southampton Waters, the effluent of the river Itchen. In this voyage, as the Map will show, the north-eastern shores of the Isle of Wight, with Ryde, Osborne, and Cowes, are clearly seen. The eye is never weary of the interesting objects on either side.

There is scarcely a town in any part of England so full of varied interest as Southampton. The beauty of its lovely situation and environs, and the delightful access to it from the Solent, make it a scene of luxury to the lover of nature ; whilst its share in English History, and the existing remains which almost at every step remind us of that history, endear it to the antiquary and the patriot. The lovers of Shakespeare need not to be reminded of the embarkation, from this port, of our most heroic sovereign to the scene of war in France, which culminated in the great victory of Agincourt, as it is vividly depicted in the first act of the great poet's " Henry the Fifth."

On the other hand, the commercial importance of this flourishing town renders it equally interesting to those who are more concerned with the present than the past. Its fine public buildings, and especially its extensive docks, are objects of great interest in this point of view.

Southampton is the largest steam-packet port in the United Kingdom, being the place of arrival and departure of the splendid fleet of vessels belonging to the Peninsular and Oriental Steam Navigation Company, the Royal West India

Mail Steam Packet Company, and other companies of great importance.

The ancient part of the town was surrounded by an embattled wall about one mile and a half in circumference, having several gates and posterns, the principal being the Bar Gate in High Street, which is a large and handsome tower gateway, retaining much of its ancient appearance.

There are many ancient framed timber houses, which have a venerable and picturesque appearance. The quays, docks, churches, the Guildhall over the Bar Gate, the cemetery, the Hartley Institute, Thorne's Almshouses, and many other objects worthy of inspection, are too numerous to be fully described.

Passing over the floating bridge that crosses the Itchen, we soon arrive at the justly celebrated ruins of Netley Abbey, the finest monastic ruin in the South of England, dedicated to St. Mary and St. Edward the Confessor, built in the Transition style of early English architecture. Many parts of the ruins are still lofty and finely mantled with ivy; the east window still retains part of its elaborate tracery, and is one of the finest examples in existence. The great Military Hospital at Netley should also be visited; the first stone was laid by Her Majesty in 1856, and has cost the nation more than £300,000.

Our return journey, for variety, may be made by the South Western Railway to Havant and Hayling. On our return journey we pass

BISHOP'S WALTHAM—a small but pleasant market town. This place is interesting, not only from its position and local peculiarities, but historically as having, from time immemorial, belonged to the See of Winchester, from which the Episcopal portion of its name is derived. A castle built here by Henry de Blois, brother of King Stephen, was demolished during the Civil Wars by the Parliamentary Army. The site of these ruins, and the several pleasant seats and mansions, will repay the tourist FOR A DAYS ramble.

Ninth Day.

Winchester and its Vicinity.

The excursion to Winchester takes us further from our starting point than any upon which we have yet ventured, but the railway communication is direct (a change of carriage only being required) from Hayling to the Cathedral City, and the journey to and fro can be accomplished in a day, with ample time to appreciate the points we have now to notice.

WINCHESTER is one of the most ancient and remarkable towns in England. It was occupied in succession by the Britons, Romans, and Saxons, having been the capital, first of the Saxon King of this district, and afterwards when Egbert became Monarch of Heptarchy, the capital of all England. This rank it maintained till after the Norman Conquest. William I., who enjoyed the pleasures of the chase afforded by the New Forest and its neighbourhood, resided at Winchester; and when his son Rufus, who inherited his taste for these pursuits, fell by the treacherous arrow of the archer, his body was interred in Winchester Cathedral, the spot being still marked by a plain contemporary monument. Under Henry I. Winchester attained its highest greatness. The standards of weights and measures for the kingdom were regulated here, and corn is still sold by "the Winchester" (meaning the Winchester bushel) in South Wales and other distant parts of the kingdom. London, however, as the metropolis of England, soon asserted its supremacy; but the great monastic establishment, founded long anterior to the Conquest, continued to give importance to Winchester, and its Cathedral, the work of successive centuries, will always render it worthy of study and admiration. The total length of Winchester Cathedral is 545 feet. The west front is imposing in its magnificence, and the long perspective of its grand interior is unequalled in England, and scarcely surpassed in Europe. The Cathedral abounds in specimens of Norman architecture, and, besides the tomb of Rufus, there are elaborate and gorgeous chantry chapels in memory of Bishops Edynton, William of Wykeham, Waynflete, and Fox. Various ancient remains of sculpture, paintings, &c., are now to be seen in a perfect state.

The famous College of Winchester, founded by William of Wykeham in 1387, and the remains of Wolvesey Castle, have many attractions for the antiquary; and the cross in the High Street, restored a few years since, is a light and elegant structure of open arches, with pinnacles, niches, and canopies.

The Hospital of ST. CROSS, about a mile to the south of Winchester, is a curious relic of munificent charity of former days. It is an extensive fabric, founded in 1136 by Henry de Blois, Bishop of Winchester, as a retreat for thirteen poor men past their strength, and to provide a dinner daily for one hundred other poor men. All travellers are yet entitled to a glass of ale and a small loaf at the Hospital gate. There is a large church attached to the establishment, which is not only beautiful in itself, but affords striking illustrations of the transition from the Norman to the Early-English styles of architecture.

We may here mention, amongst the many attractions worthy of the tourist's attention, the Assize Court (on the west end wall of the County Hall is that great curiosity called King Arthur's Round Table; it is built of oak, and is 18ft. in diameter, and is perforated by bullets in several places), the County Prison, the Market House, Hyde Abbey, the City Cross, Winchester College, the several Churches, Hospitals, &c., &c.

ROMSEY ABBEY, near Winchester, is another fine specimen of old church architecture, the greater portion of it being of the Saxon era, with rich mouldings, corbels, &c. It belonged to an establishment of Benedictine nuns, founded in the reign of Edward the Elder.

Tenth Day.

PORTCHESTER CASTLE.—As we dare not assume that, even in the most favourable season our climate can afford, each day in a brief fortnight's sojourn at Hayling Island will be available for a long or laborious excursion, we will now suggest a visit to this famous relic of antiquity, which, as it is only seven miles distant from Hayling Island, by the South Western Railway, can be visited in less time, and with less fatigue, than some of the other places included in our daily programme.

The points of interest to be here considered have been so well stated by the Rev. E. Kell, of Southampton, in a paper read to the members of the South of England Literary, Philosophical, and Statistical Society, that we need no apology for quoting them at length, as follows :—

"In giving a brief account of the locality and history of Portchester Castle, I must premise that there are no striking incidents to chain your attention. Its history does not abound in bold adventure, long sieges, sallies of the garrison, and marvellous exploits of defenders or assailants, but it is a simple narrative of a fine old fortification, passing from the possession of one people to another with the progress of political events in the country of which it formed a part. It lays a claim, however, to great antiquity. Stowe states 'that tradition reporteth it as an old British fortress called Caer Pelvis, formed by Gurgunstus, a son of Belin, in 375 B.C.,' and doubtless its situation on a tongue of land jutting into the lake in a south-easterly direction would easily point out to the inhabitants the advantages of its position as a place of defence. Its name of Portchester is obviously of Roman origin, derived from Portus and Castra. It was the great port of the harbour to this part of the English coast, and was the Portus Magnus of the Roman Itineranes. From it a road went to Clausentum and Winchester on the west, and another to Chichester on the east. It is said to have been the port at which Vespasian landed, who, in A.D. 63, reduced twenty towns in this part of the kingdom and the Isle of Wight to subjection. In that early period the sea more deeply encircled it, and a Roman fleet might ride safely on its waters. The gradual decay of Portchester is attributed to the partial desertion of the waters, which, on the other hand, led to the rise and prosperity of the neighbouring town of Portsmouth. The change in modern warfare also contributed to its decline, rendering it unavailable for purposes of warlike defence. We have no record of any events during the Roman occupation, and little that can be depended on in Saxon times. The Saxon chief Portha landed here in 501, and with his sons Biot and Megla, made himself master of the country, founding the kingdom of Wessex, and no doubt using this fortress for the support of his power. It is very uncertain, however, whether any portion of the present building can be referred to Saxon times. We have no positive information of its state till we come to the great storehouse of local knowledge, Doomsday Book, in which an account is given of Portchester, which is described simply as " Aula," a hall, and its manor is valued at £6. But no mention is made of a keep. From this circumstance, and the style of its architecture, it is considered to be of Norman construction, and was probably built in the time of King Stephen or one of the first two Henrys, when so many other castles of the country were erected. Portchester Castle was built after the usual form of Roman fortifications— quadrangular. It is 612 feet on the north and south sides, and 610 on the east and west sides. The east and south sides front the sea, and were thus protected by it from attack. The west and north sides were defended by a strong vallum and a fosse, which still admits the water at high tide. The usual width of the Roman wall which surrounds the area is six feet, and height fifteen feet, having a passage round it which once was complete. There are eighteen circular towers, of different sizes, constructed on the wall, including those of the keep. There are two entrances to this Roman fortification, one on the west and another opposite to it on the east, now surmounted by Norman towers in a state of decay, and there were two sally-ports. Connected with the old water spouts on the east side of the west entrance are the relics of two time-worn figures, something like Egyptian Sphinxes. The present towers, constructed at the east and west entrances, contained apartments for the accommodation of the guards of the fortress, and are of Norman origin. The construction of the walls should be observed, as characteristic of the Roman mode of building in bonding courses. It was customary with this people to insert, at certain intervals, layers of tiles between the stones of the wall to give it more stability. In the instance of Portchester the bonding stones are formed of a coarse limestone, instead of tile, in this particular resembling the walls of Silchester, as well as in the composition of the cement employed in the construction. From the alteration of the walls in successive periods, and from the inroads of time, irregularity prevails in the present construction of the walls, and the bonding courses cannot always be traced. The best places for seeing the arrangement of the bonded courses are in parts of the northern and southern sides. The keep is built in the form of a parallelogram, 65 feet by 115 feet. Its walls are 7 feet 4 inches thick. It consists of four storeys; the upper room has four small Norman windows, and was probably the principal apartment of the constable or governor of Portchester. The other storeys are lighted by loop windows, only large enough, one would think, to make 'darkness visible.' Yet this place was frequently occupied by royal personages, and it well indicates the poorness of their domestic accommodation. It was settled on Queen Margaret as a part of her dower by Edward the First. The two dungeons in the basement are 40 feet long, and are separated by a wall, which runs up the centre of the keep, dividing it into two parts. In this respect it resembles the keeps of the Castles of Rochester, Colchester, Dover, and Castle Rising. The exterior is faced with Caen stone, carefully dressed in regularly-sized blocks. The Royal arms are visible over the entrance to the dungeon. From the top of the keep a most commanding view may be obtained of the whole port, embracing Portsdown Hill, the adjacent towns of Gosport and Portsmouth, Spithead, the Isle of Wight, and extending eastward as far as the spire of Chichester Cathedral. In approaching the keep from the outer ballium, you pass through the barbican, in which were massive gates, two portcullises, and the place of barricade, altogether amounting to 114 feet, before the inner ballium is reached. In this part, now called the Norman Court, are a number of buildings supposed to be erected for the accommodation of the constables of the fort, and their attendants, which are of various ages, from the early Norman to the time of Henry the Eighth. On the south of the Norman Court is what is considered to have been the banqueting hall. On the west of it is Queen Elizabeth's drawing room, and on the north-east is her tower. On the east of the court the barons' hall is situated, of the date of the early part of the 16th century. The parish church, dedicated to St. Mary, is situated on the outer ballium, towards the south-east, and is conjectured to have been the Sacellum of the Roman Prætorium, a not unusual appropriation of the sacred precincts of Roman usage. It was built by Henry the First in 1133, and was originally intended for the Augustinian monks; but as the monks and the soldiers of the garrison were not likely to be the best friends, in twenty years the monastery was removed to Southwick. The structure of the church was cruciform, with a low tower at the intersection. The south transept has been removed, if it ever were completed, and other alterations have taken place in the reign of Queen Anne, whose benefactions to the church are recorded in the interior, under her Royal arms. The Norman character of the edifice is observable in the circular doors and windows, and in the zigzag and other ornaments. Unfortunately, a portion of the great west window is blocked up, but the part which remains and the doors are rich specimens of the Norman style. Within the church, at the east, is a monument of Sir Thomas Cornwallis Groom, porter to Elizabeth and James the First, painted in vermillion colour, and a curious Norman font, on which on one side is represented the baptism of our Saviour. Portchester Castle was a favourite place of residence of King John. Edward the Second also visited it several times. Edward the First and Henry the Third had some intercourse with it. Queen Elizabeth several times held her Court at Portchester."

Eleventh Day.

Although the distance to Salisbury is somewhat considerable, the visitor to Hayling has the means of direct access by railway from Hayling and Havant, and a visit to the famed Cathedral town may well be one of the many excursions he may advantageously take.

SALISBURY CATHEDRAL is a most complete and perfect specimen of early English architecture. It contains a monumental brass to the memory of John Britton, the historian of the English Cathedrals, who was accustomed to declare that this was, in his opinion, the most beautiful of them all. It has a nave and choir with two side aisles, and a lady chapel at the east end a large transept with an eastern aisle, and a smaller transept to the eastward of the former, a north porch, beautiful cloisters, and a fine chapter house. The spire is 404 feet in height (being the loftiest in England), and of surpassing beauty.

Twelfth Day.

To Portsmouth by Road.—As in previous excursions Portsmouth has been reached from Hayling, either by railway or by the west ferry and Southsea, it must not be forgotten that there is a very agreeable mode of getting there by road. Passing up West Street out of Havant and emerging into the open country, we reach first the village of Bedhampton. The Roman Catholic Church was built in 1875, at a cost of £3,000; it is an elegant Gothic structure, and contains a magnificent altar and fine organ.

The Water Works are very extensive, and supply Portsmouth, Southsea, Cosham, Havant, and Emsworth with water; the engine and boiler-house is substantially built of stone and red brick, and contains three engines, each 90 horse power. The springs, collecting ponds, and reservoirs occupy an area of seven acres.

The Church of St. Thomas is constructed in the Norman and Early-English style; the east window is filled in with stained glass, representing the Crucifixion.

The Manor House is an old brick mansion, presumed to form part of a nunnery, from which an underground passage is said to have led to the church—the residence of J. Hopkins, Esq. There are several charming seats commanding picturesque views of land and water. We must pass through Farlington (it having been previously alluded to) into Cosham, situate at the foot of Portsdown Hill.

East Court is a handsome mansion, with very beautiful grounds, occupied by Lord William Seymour, A.D.C. Wymering is but half a mile from Cosham; the church is an ancient Norman structure, dedicated to St. Peter and St. Paul, restored in 1862 at the cost of £2,000, chiefly defrayed by the Rev. — Nugee and his family; the festival of Crowning the May Queen is here celebrated in all its ancient pomp.

We now pass over Fort Bridge and through the Hilsea Fortifications, the outer defences of Portsmouth, into Portsea Island.

The Parish Church, dedicated to St. Mary, is about one mile from Portsea, and built in the time of Edward III.; it was nearly all taken down and rebuilt in 1889. Here are entombed the remains of many of those who went down in the Royal George, at Spithead, August 29th, 1782, when 700 men were supposed to be drowned. A monument also records the loss of the Hero and 600 men.

Within a short distance, substantial, though dull looking, stands the New Gaol, the boundary wall enclosing $5\frac{1}{2}$ acres, with accommodation for 104 males and 52 females, erected at a cost of £36,000.

The Union Workhouse is a large building, erected in 1845, at a cost of £20,000; it has room for 1,450 inmates.

Wending our way to the ferry at Cumberland Fort, we pass through the very pretty village of Milton. Here is a small but neat church, built in the Norman style in 1841. We can now either return viâ Portsmouth or by the ferry boat.

Thirteenth Day.

Steamboat trip round the Isle of Wight.

From the month of June to the end of September there is every opportunity of enjoying a trip by steamer completely round the Isle of Wight, and to those who delight in a pleasant, short, and safe sea voyage, there cannot be a greater treat than this affords. We must take the first train to Portsmouth to be in time for the boat.

The beautiful climate of the Isle of Wight, where laurels, myrtles, and the most delicate evergreens flourish throughout the winter; the cliffs on the southern and south-eastern coasts so interesting to the geologist, its lovely inland scenery and pleasant towns, are all too well known to need more than passing reference.   During this charming sea voyage, we pass Spithead, Ryde, Brading Harbour,* Shanklin and its beautiful Chine, Dunnose (which will ever record the loss of the Eurydice and her gallant crew).

Bonchurch, the most southern railway station in England, Chale Bay and Blackgang Chine, Freshwater Bay, the Needles, Alum Bay, Hurst Castle, Yarmouth, and Cowes. The Royal Palace of Osborne, the Church at Whippingham, and the Castle at Carisbrooke, are important and interesting features in this favoured little Island, and with the Regattas of the Royal Yacht Squadron, in the autumn at Cowes, are sources of the greatest possible attraction.

Fourteenth Day.

Having previously made arrangements with one of the boatmen on the beach, we commence our trip round Hayling Island. Entering the harbour, we pass Cumberland Fort (previously alluded to), Hayling Ferry, the site of the long-looked-for and talked-of floating bridge ; the Great Salterns of Portsea, mentioned in the Domesday Book ; Lord Nelson's monument, and the forts, situated on Portsdown Hill ; the South of England Oyster Company's works ; Langston, with its bridge communicating to Hayling Island ; the interesting church and ruins at Warblington ; Emsworth, its ship yards and rope works ; Thorney Island, and its quaint old church, well worthy of the excursionist's attention. Passing Wittering and the Coastguard Station, we sail pleasantly

----

* Destined in a few years to be the chief communication to the Isle of Wight from Hayling Island, by the London and Brighton Railway Company's route.

through the mouth of Chichester Harbour, and once more reach our happy Island home.

It is scarcely probable that all the excursions I have shown to be practicable will often be undertaken by any free-born Briton, residing for the short space of a fortnight at Hayling. My object has been to show how great and varied are some of the attractions presented by the works of nature and art, within a reasonable distance of this place. They cannot be exhausted in a fortnight; they will repay repeated visits, and they are but a few of the many attractions which render the neighbourhood of Hayling a desirable permanent abode to all those who can find

> Sermons in stones,
> Books in the running brooks,
> And good in everything.

INDEX.

EXCURSIONS.

W. W. BLAKE,

BUILDER AND CONTRACTOR,

UNDERTAKER,

PLUMBER, PAINTER AND DECORATOR.

VENETIAN AND OTHER BLINDS FITTED AND REPAIRED.

Estimates given for all descriptions of work free of charge.

OFFICE AND WORKS,

CHURCH ROAD, HAYLING.

SAMUEL JONES,

FAMILY GROCER & GENERAL WAREHOUSEMAN,

MAGDALA HOUSE,

(CLOSE TO THE POST OFFICE)

HAYLING ISLAND.

FAMILIES WAITED ON. ORDERS PUNCTUALLY ATTENDED TO, SCHOOL TREATS CATERED FOR.

YOUR PATRONAGE IS RESPECTFULLY SOLICITED.

E. TWINE,

𝔅𝔲𝔱𝔠𝔥𝔢𝔯,

❋ SEA FRONT, ❋

SOUTH HAYLING.

DAIRY FED PORK,
PICKLED TONGUES,
SOUTHDOWN MUTTON, &c.

Families waited upon daily and supplied on the most reasonable terms.

HAYLING GAS WORKS,

H. R. TRIGG,

Proprietor.

ESTIMATES GIVEN FOR GAS FITTINGS.

A large Stock on hand for selection.

COAL AND COKE WHARF.

A GOOD SUPPLY OF THE BEST

SEABORNE AND INLAND COAL

DELIVERED AT

CURRENT PRICES.

H. R. TRIGG,

AUCTIONEER & SURVEYOR,

House, Land and Estate Agent's Office,

OPPOSITE RAILWAY STATION, SOUTH HAYLING, HANTS.

BUILDING SURVEYOR TO THE HAVANT RURAL SANITARY AUTHORITY.

DESIGNS AND ESTIMATES PREPARED.

TITHES AND RENTS COLLECTED.

AGENT TO THE PHŒNIX FIRE OFFICE.

INSURANCES EFFECTED AGAINST FIRE
On all descriptions of Property.

Accidents or Death,
From any cause, either on land or water.

On HORSES against death by accident or disease.

FARM LIVE STOCK: Cattle, Sheep, Pigs, &c.

Growing Crops,
Against destruction by hail.

Vehicles
Either Carriages, Broughams, Wagons, Carts, &c., from accidents.

Plate and other Glass
From accident and malicious breakage.

THE HAVANT PRINTING OFFICE.

T. SUTER,

GENERAL PRINTER,

WEST STREET, HAVANT.

PRINTING.

BUSINESS Memorandums, Cards, Circulars, Note Headings, Invoices, Hand Bills, &c., neatly printed.

AUCTIONEERS' Posters, Catalogues, Particulars and Conditions of Sale, &c., printed on the shortest notice.

FRIENDLY SOCIETIES' Rules, Circulars, Contribution Cards, Anniversary Bills and Notices, &c., cheaply executed.

PROGRAMMES (Fancy and Plain)—Menus, Circulars, Invitations, &c., printed in colours, on the shortest notice.

Note Paper headed with any address, and in any colour, without charge for Die.

GEORGE GALE & Co.,
LIMITED,
PALE ALE BREWERS,
HORNDEAN.

Description.	Brl.	Kild.	Fkn.	Pins.
East India Pale Ale	6c	...	...	...
Pale Ale. B.B.B	54	27 —	13 6	6 9
B.B	48/	24/—	12/—	6/—
B	36 —	18 —	9 —	4 6
Double Diamond	72 —	36 —	18 —	9 —
Extra Strong Mild Ale	54 —	27 —	13 6	6 9
Strong Mild Ale	48	24/—	12	6/—
Pale Ale	42 —	21/—	10 6	5/3
Mild XX	36 —	18 —	9	4/6
Double Stout	54 —	27 —	13 6	6 9
Single Stout	48 —	24/—	12/	6/—
Porter	36 —	18 —	9 —	4 6

The B Ale, at One Shilling per Gallon is very highly recommended, being brewed specially for the use of Private Families.

In Bottle, Imperial Pints.

Golden Tonic	2 6 per doz.
East India Pale Ale	3 6 ,, ,,
Nourishing Stout	2 6 ,, ,,

Delivery by our own Vans in the Island.

W. LENG,

CABINET MAKER AND UPHOLSTERER,

Appraiser and House Agent,

CARPET AND GENERAL FURNISHING WAREHOUSE,

EAST STREET, HAVANT.

A LARGE STOCK

OF

ANTIQUE, OAK, MAHOGANY, SATINWOOD AND INLAID FURNITURE,

OLD CHINA AND CURIOS

IN STOCK.

WILLIAM SCORER,

NORTH STREET, HAVANT.

DEALER IN

PHOTOGRAPHIC APPARATUS, CHEMICALS,

AND ALL KINDS OF

APPLIANCES FOR AMATEURS.

A DARK ROOM.

LOCAL VIEWS IN GREAT VARIETY. PORTRAITS. VIEWS AND GROUPS TAKEN.

LOCAL AGENT FOR VIEWS:—

Mr. W. J. ROWE, THE BEACH, SOUTH HAYLING.

The negatives for the Collotypes in this Book were taken by William Scorer.

The "ROYAL HOTEL,"
HAYLING ISLAND.

EXCELLENT ACCOMMODATION.

Commanding a Magnificent Sea View. Beautiful Beach and Sands. Splendid Bathing.

THE FINEST GOLFING GROUND IN THE SOUTH OF ENGLAND.

Excellent Train Service by the London and South Coast Railway from
VICTORIA & LONDON BRIDGE STATIONS,
Or by the London and South Western Railway from
WATERLOO STATION.

Omnibuses meet all Trains at Hayling Station.

APPLY TO MANAGER.

The South Hants Mineral Water Manufactory.

WHITE & CHIGNELL'S
Aerated Waters

Are prepared with a direct and fresh supply (twice daily) of the now celebrated Brockampton Spring Water; which is afterwards filtered through Charcoal Filters, and is thus rendered absolutely pure and wholesome.

The purest chemicals are used in the manufacture, and an uniform quantity in each bottle may be depended on.

AERATED WATER—Price 1s. 6d. per doz.

SODA WATER—is valuable as an antacid, and for table water for use at meals. Price 1s. 6d. per doz.

SELTZER WATER—a valuable dietetic and aid to digestion. Price 2s. 6d. per doz.

POTASS WATER—highly recommended by the faculty when an alkaline effervescence is required. Price 2s. 6d. per doz.

LEMONADE—pure and delicate in flavour. Price 1s. 6d. per doz.

GINGER BEER—warranted not to contain cream of tartar or any other injurious chemical. Price 1s. 6d. per doz.

All the above waters are bottled in the New Glass Stoppered bottles, which are easily opened, and half the contents can be used at one time.

DELIVERED TWICE DAILY IN HAYLING.

Orders received at Branch Shop, close to Gas Works.

CPSIA information can be obtained at www.ICGtesting.com
Printed in the USA
BVOW07s1708280414

351936BV00012B/683/P

9 781241 318567